THE

# REALM OF ESSENCE

BOOK FIRST

OF

## REALMS OF BEING

BY

GEORGE SANTAYANA

NEW YORK

CHARLES SCRIBNER'S SONS

*First Published* 1927

*Printed in Great Britain by* R. & R. CLARK, LIMITED, *Edinburgh.*

# PREFACE TO REALMS OF BEING

THE world is old, and can have changed but little since
man arose in it, else man himself would have perished.
Why, then, should he still live without a sure and
sufficient philosophy? The equivalent of such a philosophy is probably hereditary in sundry animals not
much older than man. They have had time to take
the measure of life, and have settled down to a routine
of preferences and habits which keeps their heads, as a
race, above water; and they are presumably visited at
appropriate seasons by magic images, which are symbols
to them for the world or for the cycles of their destiny.
Among groups of men an equilibrium of this moral
sort has been sometimes approached—in India, in
China, under the Moslem or the Catholic regimens;
and if socialist or other panaceas now exercise such a
strange influence over men's hearts, it is perhaps
because they are impatient of being so long the sport
of divers ignorant dogmas and chance adventures, and
aspire to live in a stable harmony with nature.

In fact, beneath these various complete systems
which have professed but failed to be universal, there
is actually a dumb human philosophy, incomplete but
solid, prevalent among all civilised peoples. They all
practise agriculture, commerce, and mechanical arts,
with artificial instruments lately very much complicated; and they necessarily possess, with these arts, a
modicum of sanity, morality, and science requisite for

carrying them on, and tested by success in doing so. Is not this human competence philosophy enough? Is it not at least the nucleus of all sound philosophy? In spite of the superficial confusion reigning in the world, is not the universal wisdom of the future actually gathering about this human competence in engineering, in chemistry, in medicine, in war?

It might seem so, since the sort of knowledge involved in the arts, though it may not go very far, is The realm compulsory so far as it goes, and being of matter. sanctioned by success, it ought to be permanent and progressive. There is indeed a circle of material events called nature, to which all minds belonging to the same society are responsive in common. Not to be responsive to these facts is simply to be stupid and backward in the arts; those who explore and master their environment cannot help learning what it is. In this direction competence involves enlightenment. Among minds forming a moral society, and able to compare their several opinions, this enlightenment in the expert is coercive over the layman also, because the same facts confront them both. Did not the same facts confront them, communication would be impossible between them, or if communication was reputed to exist by magic there would be no possible conflict or progress among their opinions, because they would not refer to the same events. Even if each declared himself competent and prosperous in his own world, he would know nothing of the world of his neighbours. Their several minds would simply be variously or similarly brilliant, like jewels, signifying nothing to one another.

If any mind hopes to address another (or even itself) persuasively, as I now wish to address the reader and my own thoughts, it must assume a single system of events to which both minds are responsive, and which includes their respective bodies and actions.

Assuming such a common world, it is easy to see how animals may acquire knowledge of it and may communicate it.   Material events will arouse in them intuitions conformable to their several stations, faculties, and passions; and their active nature (since they are animals, not plants) will compel them to regard many of the essences so given in intuition as signs for the environment in which they move, modifying this environment and affected by it.   This assumption justifies itself at every turn in practice, and establishes in the habits of all men, in proportion to their competence, an appropriate adjustment to the *Realm of Matter*, and in their imagination a suitable picture of the same.

Nevertheless, since the station, faculties, and passions of all men are not identical, these pictures will not be similar.   Different observers may be The realm addressed to different regions of nature, or of essence. sensitive to different elements in the same region; thus dwellers in distinct planets must evidently have distinct geographies, and the same battle in the clouds will be known to the deaf only as lightning and to the blind only as thunder, each responding to a different constituent of the total event, and not simultaneously.   So an eclipse—itself but one aspect of a constellation of events in the heavens—may be known in various entirely different terms; by calculation before it occurs, by sense when it is occurring, by memory immediately afterwards, and by reports to posterity.   All these indications are entirely inadequate to the facts they reveal in the realm of matter, and qualitatively unlike those facts; they are a set of variegated symbols by which sensitive animals can designate them.   Of course, the existence and use of such languages is an added fact in nature—a fact so important and close to the egotism of the animals themselves as perhaps to obscure all else in their eyes. Their instinct, indeed, keeps their attention stretched upon the material world that actually surrounds them; but sometimes sensation and language, instead of being passed over like the ticking of the telegraph, may become objects in themselves, in all their absolute musical insignificance; and then animals become idealists. The terms in which they describe things, unlike the things they meant to describe, are purely specious, arbitrary, and ideal; whether visual, tactile, auditory, or conceptual these terms are essentially *words*. They possess intrinsically, in their own ontological plane, only logical or æsthetic being; and this contains no indication whatever of the material act of speaking, touching, or looking which causes them to appear. All possible terms in mental discourse arc essences existing nowhere; visionary equally, whether the faculty that discovers them be sense or thought or the most fantastic fancy.

Such diversity in animal experience taken in itself exhibits sundry qualities or forms of being, a part of the infinite multitude of distinguishable ideal terms which (whether ever revealed to anybody or not) I call the *Realm of Essence*. Pure intuition, in its poetic ecstasy, would simply drink in such of these essences as happened to present themselves; but for a wakeful animal they are signals. They report to his spirit, in very summary and uncertain images, the material events which surround him and which concern his welfare. They may accordingly become terms in knowledge if interpreted judiciously, and if interpreted injudiciously they may become illusions.

The dumb philosophy of the human animal, by which he rears his family and practises the arts and All mental finds his way home, might take definite shape discourse is and establish a healthy routine in all his dealmore or less ings with matter (which includes society), significant and yet his imaginative experience might poetry. retain all its specious originality. The control which the environment exercises over the structure and conduct of animals is decidedly loose. They can live dragging a long chain of idle tricks, diseases, and obsolete organs; and even this loose control fails almost entirely in the case of alternative senses or languages, one of which may serve as well as another. Many species survive together, many rival endowments and customs and religions. And the same control fails altogether in regard to the immaterial essences which those senses or languages call up before the mind's eye. Adaptation is physical, and it is only the material operation in sensation or speech that can possibly be implicated in the clockwork of nature. The choice of those visionary essences which meantime visit the mind, though regular, is free; they are the transcript of life into discourse, the rhetorical and emotional rendering of existence, which when deepened and purified, becomes poetry or music. There can be no reason why differences in these spheres, even among men of the same race, should not be perpetual. It would be mere sluggishness and egotism to regret it. Such differences are not merely added like a vain luxury to a sane recognition, in other conscious terms, of the facts of nature. The "sane" response to nature is by action only and by an economy which nature can accept and weave into her own material economy; but as to the terms of sense and discourse, they are all from the very beginning equally arbitrary, poetical, and (if you choose) mad; yet all equally symptomatic. They vary initially and intangibly from mind to mind, even in expressing the same routine of nature. The imagination which eventually runs to fine art or religion is the same faculty which, under a more direct control of external events, yields vulgar perception. The promptings and the control exercised by matter are continuous in both cases; the dream requires a material dreamer as much as the waking sensation, and the latter

*b*

is a transcript of his bodily condition just as directly
as the dream. Poetic, creative, original fancy is not a
secondary form of sensibility, but its first and only
form. The same manual restlessness and knack which
makes man a manufacturer of toys makes him, when
by chance his toys prove useful, a manufacturer of
implements. Fine art is thus older than servile labour,
and the poetic quality of experience is more fundamental than its scientific value. Existence may revert
at any moment to play, or may run down in idleness;
but it is impossible that any work or discovery should
ever come about without the accompaniment of pure
contemplation, if there is consciousness at all; so that
the inherent freedom of the spirit can never be stamped
out, so long as spirit endures.

Nor is it safe to imagine that inspired people,
because they dream awake in their philosophy,
The realm must come to grief in the real world. The
of spirit. great religious and political systems which
I mentioned above have had brilliant careers. Their
adepts have been far from making worse soldiers than
sceptics make, or worse workmen than materialists;
nor have they committed suicide or been locked up in
the madhouse more often than exact philosophers.
Nature drives with a loose rein, and vitality of any sort,
even if expressed in fancy, can blunder through many
a predicament in which reason would despair. And
if the mythical systems decline at last, it is not so much
by virtue of the maladjustments underlying their speculative errors—for their myths as a whole are wisely
contrived—as because imagination in its freedom
abandons these errors for others simply because the
prevalent mood of mankind has changed, and it begins
dreaming in a different key. Spirit bloweth where it
listeth, and continually undoes its own work. This
world of free expression, this drift of sensations, passions, and ideas, perpetually kindled and fading in the

light of consciousness, I call the *Realm of Spirit*. It is only for the sake of this free life that material competence and knowledge of fact are worth attaining. Facts for a living creature are only instruments; his play-life is his true life. On his working days, when he is attentive to matter, he is only his own servant, preparing the feast. He becomes his own master in his holidays and in his sportive passions. Among these must be counted literature and philosophy, and so much of love, religion, and patriotism as is not an effort to survive materially. In such enthusiasms there is much asseveration; but what they attest is really not the character of the external facts concerned, but only the spiritual uses to which the spirit turns them.

A philosopher cannot wish to be deceived. His philosophy is a declaration of policy in the presence of the facts; and therefore his first care must be to ascertain and heartily to acknowledge all such facts as are relevant to his action or sentiment—not less, and not necessarily more. The range of reasonable curiosity. The pursuit of truth is a form of courage, and a philosopher may well love truth for its own sake, in that he is disposed to confront destiny, whatever it may be, with zest when possible, with resignation when necessary, and not seldom with amusement. The facts to which it is prudent and noble in him to bare his bosom are the morally relevant facts, such as touch his fortunes or his heart, or such as he can alter by his efforts; nor can he really discover other facts. Intuition, or absolute apprehension without media or doubt, is proper to spirit perusing essences; it is impossible to animals confronting facts. Animals know things by exploration, reaction, and prophetic fancy; they therefore can know only such parts and depths of nature as they explore materially and respond to vitally. The brave impulse to search may, indeed, become eager and may wish to recognise no limits; and there may be spirits so utterly practical and serious that the pursuit of material facts absorbs them altogether, to the exclusion of all play of mind. Yet such hectic exactitude is an expression of fear, and automatic rather than rational. Curiosity in an animal always has limits which it is foolish to transgress, because beyond them theory insensibly lapses into verbal myths, and if still taken for true knowledge defeats the honest curiosity that inspired it. What renders knowledge true is fidelity to the object; but in the conduct and fancy of an animal this fidelity can be only rough, summary, dramatic; too much refinement renders it subjective, as does too much haste. This is true of mathematical refinements no less than of verbal pedantries. The realm of matter can never be disclosed either to hypothesis or to sensation in its presumable inmost structure and ultimate extent: the garment of appearance must always fit it loosely and drape it in alien folds, because appearance is essentially an adaptation of facts to the scale and faculty of the observer.

There are also moral limits to seriousness and utter literalness in thought. The tragic compulsion to honour the facts is imposed on man by the destiny of his body, to which that of his mind is attached. But his destiny is not the only theme possible to his thought, nor the most congenial. The best part of this destiny is that he may often forget it; and existence would not be worth preserving if it had to be spent exclusively in anxiety about existence.

It follows from all this that knowledge of facts merely because they are facts cannot be the ultimate Relativity of object of a philosopher, although he must knowledge. wish to know the whole unvarnished truth about relevant matters. A liberal mind must live on its own terms, and think in them; it is not inferior to what surrounds it; fact-worship on its part would accordingly be a fault in taste and in morals. What is the function of philosophy? To disclose the absolute truth? But is it credible that the absolute truth should descend into the thoughts of a mortal creature, equipped with a few special senses and with a biassed intellect, a man lost amidst millions of his fellows and a prey to the epidemic delusions of the race? Possession of the absolute truth is not merely by accident beyond the range of particular minds; it is incompatible with being alive, because it excludes any particular station, organ, interest, or date of survey: the absolute truth is undiscoverable just because it is not a perspective. Perspectives are essential to animal apprehension; an observer, himself a part of the world he observes, must have a particular station in it; he cannot be equally near to everything, nor internal to anything but himself; of the rest he can only take views, abstracted according to his sensibility and fore-shortened according to his interests. Those animals which I was supposing endowed with an adequate philosophy surely do not possess the absolute truth. They read nature in their private idioms. Their imagination, like the human, is doubtless incapable of coping with all things at once, or even with the whole of anything natural. Mind was not created for the sake of discovering the absolute truth. The absolute truth has its own intangible reality, and scorns to be known. The function of mind is rather to increase the wealth of the universe in the spiritual dimension, by adding appearance to substance and passion to necessity, and by creating all those private perspectives, and those emotions of wonder, adventure, curiosity, and laughter which omniscience would exclude. If omniscience were alone respectable, creation would have been a mistake. The single duty of all creatures would then be to repair that creative error, by abolishing their several senses and desires and becoming indis-

THE REALM OF ESSENCE

tinguishable from one another and from nothing at all; and if all creation could attain to this sort of salvation, the absolute substance, in whose honour all else had been abandoned, would become unconscious. The time will doubtless come for each of us, if not for the universe at large, to cease from care; but our passage through life will have added a marvellous episode to the tale of things; and our distinction and glory, as well as our sorrow, will have lain in being something in particular, and in knowing what it is.

Thus if there is a sense in which all special and separable existence is illusion, there is another sense in which illusion is itself a special and separable existence; and if this be condemned for not being absolute substance and for excluding knowledge of the absolute truth, it may also be prized for these very reasons. Sensation is true enough. All experience yields some acquaintance with the realm of essence, and some perspective of the material world; and this would always be a true perspective (since things seen at that angle and with that organ really look like that) if the appearance were not stretched to cover more than it covers in reality. Of such true perspectives the simplest and most violently foreshortened may be as good as the most complicated, the most poetical or pictorial as good as the most scientific, not only æsthetically but even cognitively; because it may report the things concerned on that human scale on which we need to measure them, and in this relation may report them correctly. Nor is the error which such very partial knowledge may breed, when inflated by precipitate judgements and vanity, altogether unavoidable. The variety of senses in man, the precarious rule of his instincts, and the range of his memory and fancy, give rise in him eventually to some sense of error and even of humour. He is almost able to pierce the illusions of his animal dogmatism, to surrender the claim to

inspiration, and in one sense to transcend the relativity
of his knowledge and the flightiness of his passions by
acknowledging them with a good grace.

This relativity does not imply that there is no
absolute truth. On the contrary, if there were no
absolute truth, all-inclusive and eternal, the     The realm
desultory views taken from time to time by     of truth.
individuals would themselves be absolute. They
would be irrelevant to one another, and incom-
parable in point of truth, each being without any
object but the essence which appeared in it. If views
can be more or less correct, and perhaps complementary
to one another, it is because they refer to the same
system of nature, the complete description of which,
covering the whole past and the whole future, would
be the absolute truth. This absolute truth is no living
view, no actual judgement, but merely that segment of
the realm of essence which happens to be illustrated
in existence. The question whether a given essence
belongs to this segment or not—that is, whether a
suggested idea is or is not true—has a tragic importance
for an animal intent on discovering and describing
what exists, or has existed, or is destined to exist in his
world. He seldom has leisure to dwell on essences
apart from their presumable truth; even their beauty
and dialectical pattern seem to him rather trivial, unless
they are significant of facts in the realm of matter, controlling human destiny. I therefore give a special
name to this tragic segment of the realm of essence
and call it the *Realm of Truth*.

The knowledge of relevant truth, while it has this
fundamental moral importance, is far from being our
only concern in the life of reason. It comes     Human
in only incidentally, in so far as a staunch     values of
and comprehensive knowledge of things makes     knowledge.
a man master of things, and independent of them in a
great measure. The business of a philosopher is

rather to be a good shepherd of his thoughts. The
share of attention and weight which he gives to physical
speculation or to history or to psychology will express
his race and disposition, or the spirit of his times;
everyone is free to decide how far material arts and
sciences are worth pursuing, and with what free creations they shall be surrounded. Young and ardent
minds, and races without accumulated possessions,
tend to poetry and metaphysics; they neglect or falsify
the truth in the heat of their imaginative passion. Old
men, and old nations, incline to mix their wine with
larger dilutions of reality; and they prefer history,
biography, politics, and humorous fictions; because in
all these, while the facts are neither conceived nor
tested scientifically, the savour of earth and of experience remains dominant.

By the philosopher, however, both the homeliest
brew and the most meticulous science are only relished
as food for the spirit. Even if defeated in the pursuit
of truth, the spirit may be victorious in self-expression
and self-knowledge; and if a philosopher could be
nothing else, he might still be a moralist and a poet.
He will do well to endow his vision of things with all
the force, colour, and scope of which his soul is capable.
Then if he misses the truth of nature, as in many things
is probable, he will at least have achieved a work of
imagination. In such a case the universe, without
being mapped as a whole in the fancy, will be enriched
at one point, by the happy life enacted there, in one
human focus of art and vision. The purer and more
distinct the spirit which a philosopher can bring to
light in his thoughts, the greater the intellectual achievement; and the greater the moral achievement also, if
the policy so set forth is actually carried out in his
whole life and conversation.

As for me, in stretching my canvas and taking up
my palette and brush, I am not vexed that masters

should have painted before me in styles which I have
no power and no occasion to imitate; nor do I expect
future generations to be satisfied with always Legitimate
repainting my pictures. Agreement is sweet, variety in
being a form of friendship; it is also a speculation.
stimulus to insight, and helpful, as contradiction is not;
and I certainly hope to find agreement in some quarters.
Yet I am not much concerned about the number of
those who may be my friends in the spirit, nor do I
care about their chronological distribution, being as
much pleased to discover one intellectual kinsman in
the past as to imagine two in the future. That in
the world at large alien natures should prevail, innumerable and perhaps infinitely various, does not
disturb me. On the contrary, I hope fate may manifest to them such objects as they need and can love;
and although my sympathy with them cannot be so
vivid as with men of my own mind, and in some cases
may pass into antipathy, I do not conceive that they
are wrong or inferior for being different from me, or
from one another. If God and nature can put up
with them, why should I raise an objection? But let
them take care; for if they have sinned against the
facts (as I suspect is often the case) and are kicking
against the pricks of matter, they must expect to be
brought to confusion on the day of doom, or earlier.
Not only will their career be brief and troubled, which
is the lot of all flesh, but their faith will be stultified by
events, which is a needless and eternal ignominy for the
spirit. But if somehow, in their chosen terms, they
have balanced their accounts with nature, they are to
be heartily congratulated on their moral diversity. It
is pleasant to think that the fertility of spirit is inexhaustible, if matter only gives it a chance, and that the
worst and most successful fanaticism cannot turn the
moral world permanently into a desert.

The pity of it is only that contrary souls should often

fight for the same bodies, natural or political, as if
space and matter in the universe were inadequate (as
on earth indeed they are) for every essence in its own
time to see the sun. But existence is precipitate and
blind; it cannot bide its time; and the seeds of form
are often so wantonly and thickly scattered that they
strangle one another, call one another weeds and tares,
and can live only in the distracted effort to keep others
from living. Seldom does any soul live through a
single and lovely summer in its native garden, suffered
and content to bloom. Philosophers and nations cannot be happy unless separate; then they may be single-
minded at home and tolerant abroad. If they have a
spirit in them which is worth cultivating (which is not
always the case) they need to entrench it in some con-
secrated citadel, where it may come to perfect expression. Human beings allowed to run loose are vowed
to perdition, since they are too individual to agree and
too gregarious to stand alone. Hence the rareness of
any polity founded on wisdom, like that of which
ancient Greece affords some glimpses, and the equal
rareness of a pure and complete philosophy, such as
that of Dante or of Spinoza, conceived in some moment
of wonderful unanimity or of fortunate isolation.

My own philosophy, I venture to think, is well-
knit in the same sense, in spite of perhaps seeming
The temper   eclectic and of leaving so many doors open
of this      both in physics and in morals. My eclec-
system.      ticism is not helplessness before sundry influences; it is detachment and firmness in taking each
thing simply for what it is. Openness, too, is a form
of architecture. The doctrine that all moralities equally
are but expressions of animal life is a tremendous
dogma, at once blessing and purging all mortal passions;
and the conviction that there can be no knowledge save
animal faith positing external facts, and that this
natural science is but a human symbol for those facts,

also has an immense finality: the renunciation and the assurance in it are both radical and both invincible.

In confessing that I have merely touched the hem of nature's garment, I feel that virtue from her has passed into me, and made me whole. There is no more bewitching moment in childhood than when the boy, to whom someone is slyly propounding some absurdity, suddenly looks up and smiles. The brat has understood. A thin deception was being practised on him, in the hope that he might not be deceived, but by deriding it might prove he had attained to a man's stature and a man's wit. It was but banter prompted by love. So with this thin deception practised upon me by nature. The great Sphinx in posing her riddle and looking so threatening and mysterious is secretly hoping that I may laugh. She is not a riddle but a fact; the words she whispers are not oracles but prattle. Why take her residual silence, which is inevitable, for a challenge or a menace? She does not know how to speak more plainly. Her secret is as great a secret to herself as to me. If I perceive it, and laugh, instantly she draws in her claws. A tremor runs through her enigmatical body; and if she were not of stone she would embrace her boyish discoverer, and yield herself to him altogether. It is so simple to exist, to be what one is for no reason, to engulf all questions and answers in the rush of being that sustains them. Henceforth nature and spirit can play together like mother and child, each marvellously pleasant to the other, yet deeply unintelligible; for as she created him she knew not how, merely by smiling in her dreams, so in awaking and smiling back he somehow understands her; at least he is all the understanding she has of herself.

# CONTENTS

Ἔστιν . . . πρῶτον διαιρετέον τάδε· τί τὸ ὂν ἀεί, γένεσιν δὲ οὐκ ἔχον . . . ἀεὶ κατὰ ταὐτὰ ὄν.—The first distinction to make is this: What is that which always is, having no origin, and being always identical with itself?—PLATO.

Buddha teaches that all beings are from eternity abiding in Nirvana.—Dasgupta's *History of Indian Philosophy*.

Per Deum intelligo ens absolute infinitum, hoc est, substantiam constantem infinitis attributis, quorum unumquodque aeternam et infinitam essentiam exprimit. . . . Quod autem absolute infinitum est, ad ejus essentiam pertinet quidquid essentiam exprimit.— By God I understand Being absolutely infinite, that is, substance consisting of infinitely numerous attributes, each of which expresses eternal and infinite essence . . . For if a thing is absolutely infinite, whatsoever expresses any essence belongs to the essence of that thing.—SPINOZA.

Le néant . . . est infini; il est éternel; il a bien des attributs communs avec Dieu; il comprend une infinité de choses, car toutes celles qui ne sont point sont comprises dans le néant, et celles qui ne sont plus sont rentrées dans le néant.—The Non-existent . . . is infinite, it is eternal; it possesses many attributes in common with God; it includes an infinity of things since all those which never exist belong to the Non-existent, and those which exist no longer have fallen back into the Non-existent.—LEIBNIZ.

# THE REALM OF ESSENCE

# CHAPTER I

VARIOUS APPROACHES TO ESSENCE

THE modern or romantic man is an adventurer; he is less interested in what there may be to find than in the lure of the search and in his hopes, guesses, or experiences in searching. Essence is perfectly indifferent to being discovered and unaffected by the avenue through which any discoverer may approach it; and for that very reason the explorer ignores it, and asks what it can possibly be. Now the subjective attitude in philosophy is not only prevalent in these times, but always legitimate; because a mind capable of self-consciousness is always free to reduce all things to its own view of them. Before considering the realm of essence in itself, therefore, I will indicate some paths by which even the most rambling reflection may be led to it. Essence is indeed everywhere at hand; and a scrupulous scepticism, falling back on immediate appearance, is itself a chief means of discovering the pervasive presence of essences.

*All approaches are adventitious.*

In a volume on *Scepticism and Animal Faith*, to which the present work is a sequel, I have described in detail the approach to essence through scepticism. Knowledge such as animal life requires is something transitive, a form of belief in things absent or eventual or somehow more than the state of the animal knowing them. It needs to be informa-

*Approach through scepticism: Nothing indubitable save the character of some given essence.*

I                                                         B

tion.  Otherwise the animal mind would be the prisoner of its dreams, and no better informed than a stone about its environment, its past, or its destiny.

It follows that such transitive knowledge will always be open to doubt.   It is a claim or presumption arising in a responsive organism;  yet in spite of this biological status, it ventures upon assertions concerning facts elsewhere.   This boldness exposes it to all sorts of errors;  for opinion will vary with its organ and, on that irrelevant ground, will make varying assertions about its outlying objects.   Nor is it to be presumed that initially the terms in which objects are conceived are their intrinsic qualities;  the terms may be, in quality as in existence, generated in the organ of sense, as are words or optical perspectives.   Knowledge of nature or of absent experience is accordingly no less questionable in its texture than in its scope.   Its validity is only presumptive and its terms are merely symbols.

The sceptic once on this scent will soon trace essence to its lair.   He will drop, as dubious and un-warranted, the belief in a past, an environment, or a destiny.   He will dismiss all thought of any truth to be discovered or any mind engaged in that egregious chase;  and he will honestly confine himself to noting the features of the passing apparition.   At first he may still assume that he can survey the passage and transformation of his dreams;  but soon, if he is truly sceptical and candid, he will confess that this alleged order of appearances and this extended experience are themselves only dreamt of, like the future or the remoter past or the material environment—those dis-carded idols of his dogmatic days.   Nothing will remain but some appearance now;  and that which appears, when all gratuitous implications of a world beyond or of a self here are discarded, will be an *essence*.   Nor will his own spirit, or spirit absolute (which grammar may still seem to insert, under the form of the pronoun I, as a prior agent in this intuition of essence) be anything but another name for the absolute phantom, the unmeaning presence, into which knowledge will have collapsed.

This approach to essence through scepticism is by no means the only one possible, even for a critic of knowledge. Scepticism can impugn only such knowledge as is a form of faith, and posits a removed object; but the dialectician ignores this sort of knowledge as much as he can, and by his initial attitude plants himself in the realm of essence, and wishes to confine himself to it. What is dialectic? Precisely an analysis or construction of ideal forms which abstracts from such animal faith as might be stimulated by their presence, and traces instead the inherent patterns or logical relations of these forms as intuition reveals them. To the dialectician animal faith seems wanton and superfluous, and in his overt reasoning, if not in his secret assumptions, he neither posits any objects of natural knowledge nor seeks to describe them. Such preoccupation with dark external facts and hidden events seems to him but a grovelling instinct; and the persuasion that one's ideas describe natural objects, though inevitable perhaps in sniffing one's way through this nether world, he laughs at as a vain presumption, unworthy of the name of science. In practice, as a man amongst men, the dialectician may have mixed views. If he is an enthusiast or a naturalist in disguise, using dialectic for some ulterior purpose, he will probably embrace his conclusions not merely as implications of his premises, but as objects of hot animal faith; and he may even think he has discovered a metaphysical world, when in truth he has merely elaborated a system of essences, altogether imaginary, and in no way more deeply rooted in reality than any system

*Approach through dialectic: every term intuited or defined is an essence.*

of essences which a poet or a musician might compose.
This eventual mystification, however, by which dialectic
is represented as revealing facts, does not destroy its
native competence to describe essences; in its purity
it will be free from error, because free from any
pretence to define ulterior existences.  Now this very
purity, this identity of the object envisaged with the
definition given to it in thought, seems to the dialectician
the perfection of science, because it is the last refuge of
certitude.  But certitude and dialectical cogency are
far removed from animal faith, and unnecessary to it;
and animal faith, when it describes in suitable symbols
(of which a dialectical system may be one) the objects
encountered in action, is what I call knowledge.  The
question of titles and preferences does not concern
me here; in any case the dialectician, whether his art be
called knowledge or not, has discovered the realm of
essence (or some province in it) and has devoted
himself to exploring it.

This acquaintance with essence I call intuition,
whether it be passive, æsthetic, and mystical, or on the
contrary analytical and selective, as in reasoned
discourse; because at every point demonstration or inference depends for its force on
intuition of the intrinsic relation between
the given terms.  So in planning a series of
moves in chess, as in originally inventing
that game, the mind *sees* the consequences
implied at each stage by the rules of procedure:
these rules are mere essences, but their implications
are precise in any hypothetical position of the pieces.
If chess were not a well-established game and if
material chess-boards and chess-men had never existed,
a day-dream in which particular imaginary matches
were traced out, could hardly be called knowledge:
but every possibility and every consequence involved
at each juncture would be equally definite, and the

*Distinguish-able essences, such as the terms of dialectic, are the most real of beings.*

science of chess—even if chess never had existed in the world—would be an exact science. Evidently an exact science is not without an object, ideal as this object may be: indeed, the ideal definition of that object, the absence of all ambiguity as to what it is, renders exact science of it possible. Such definable non-existent objects of exact science have being in an eminent degree; their nature and their eternal intrinsic relations to other comparable natures are perfectly determinate. They are what they are; and of all the meanings of the word *is*—existence, substance, equivalence, definition, etc., the most radical and proper is that in which I may say of anything that it is what it is. This asseveration does not commit me to any classification of the object or to any assertion of its existence. I merely note its idiosyncrasy, its qualitative identity, which enables me to distinguish it, study it, and hold it fast in my intent, so that I may eventually frame a definition of it, and perhaps assert or deny its existence. If any object had no such specific character, there would be no truth in saying that *it* was before me, or could ever again be the theme of memory or discourse. Essences, by being eternally what they are, enable existence to pass from one phase to another, and enable the mind to note and describe the change.

That what I see, I see, or what I am, I am, may seem a vain assertion: practical minds are not interested in anything except for the sake of something else. They are camp-followers or heralds of events, without self-possession. Yet if that which is actual and possessed at the moment never had a satisfying character, no satisfaction would ever be possible; the mind could never dip twice into the same subject or know its friends from its enemies, and life would be what a romantic philosophy would make it—an idle escape from one error into another. Radical flux is indeed

They are the only staunch possessions of the mind.

characteristic of existence, where it is innocent, since there can be no mistake or regret where there is no purpose: but the mind, even if describing only the series of its own illusions, attempts to describe it with truth: and it could not so much as fail in this attempt unless that series of illusions and each of its terms had a precise inexpungible character. Then the question whether in some ulterior sense those phases were illusions or not, becomes a subsidiary question. In any case, internally, they were what they were; and to a simple and recollected spirit the obvious often is enough. Its identity may have a deep charm, like that of a jewel. I may long ruminate upon it and impress it upon myself by repetitions, which to a lover never seem vain. Even in the midst of distractions, if I say to myself "No, no", or "Business is business", the repetition serves to detach and to render indubitable the essence meant; it raises that material accident to the intellectual level, where my judgement henceforth may recognise it to the exclusion of circumstances, which do not alter essences, but only cases.

Sometimes sense itself, without any dialectical analysis, distinguishes essences from facts, and recognises them in their ideal sphere. This happens for a very simple reason. The stimulus that calls animal attention to some external fact, in provoking an act of the body, also presents some image to the mind. Moreover this labour of perception may be more or less welcome, pleasant, or life-enhancing, apart from its ulterior uses; and sometimes this incidental emotion is so strong that it overpowers the interest which I may have had originally in the external facts; and, I may suspend my action or continue it automatically, while my thought is absorbed in the image and arrested there. As I was jogging to market in my village cart, beauty has burst

*Approach through contemplation: Every intelligible pattern or harmony is an essence.*

upon me and the reins have dropped from my hands.
I am transported, in a certain measure, into a state of
trance.   I see with extraordinary clearness, yet what I
see seems strange and wonderful, because I no longer
look in order to understand, but only in order to see.
I have lost my preoccupation with fact, and am contemplating an essence.

This experience, in modern times, is called æsthetic;
but it has no exclusive connection with the arts or with
the beautiful.   It is really intellectual, and the high
Platonic road.   That the clearest and purest reality
should be formal or ideal, and something on which no
animal instinct could possibly be directed, may seem a
paradox;  it may be denied by cynics—often very dull
people;   it may be used by metaphysicians as an
argument for the supernatural origin and destiny of the
soul.   It is important at once to discard any such
inferences, not only because they are in themselves
mistaken, thin, and superstitious, but particularly,
at this point in my argument, because they encumber
the notion of essence with a moral significance quite
extraneous to it, and may distort and discredit it
altogether.   When a thing is beautiful, I stop to look
at it;  and in this way its beauty helps me to Essences are
drink in the actual appearance, and to be beautiful
satisfied with that ethereal draught.   But when con-
                                                    gruous with
if the thing were ugly or uninteresting, it human
would have an absolute appearance just as faculty.
much, and would present an essence to intuition;
only that in that case I should have no motive—
no vital animal motive—for dwelling upon that essence,
or noticing it at all.   If the thing is beautiful,
this is not because it manifests an essence, but
because the essence which it manifests is one to
which my nature is attuned, so that the intuition of it
is a delightful exercise to my senses and to my soul.
This pleasure and refreshment welling up in me, I

courteously thank the object for, and call its intrinsic charm: but an intrinsic charm is a contradiction in terms, and all that the object possesses is affinity to my life, and power over it, without which it would be impossible for me to observe it or to think it beautiful.

The beautiful is itself an essence, an indefinable quality felt in many things which, however disparate they may be otherwise, receive this name by virtue of a special emotion, half wonder, half love, which is felt in their presence. The essence of the beautiful, when made an object of contemplation by itself, is rather misleading: like the good and like pure Being, it requires much dialectical and spiritual training to discern it in its purity and in its fullness. At first the impetuous philosopher, seeing the world in so many places flowering into beauty, may confuse his physics with a subjective or teleological reference to the beautiful, thereby turning this essence, which marks a spiritual consummation, into a material power: or, if he is not an enthusiast, he may dwell so much on the instinctive and pleasant bonds which attach men to what they call beautiful, that he may bury the essence of the beautiful altogether under heavy descriptions of the occasions on which perhaps it appears. I will not stop to discuss these complications: however apt to become entangled itself, the beautiful is a great liberator of other essences. The most material thing, in so far as it is felt to be beautiful, is instantly immaterialised, raised above external personal relations, concentrated and deepened in its proper being, in a word, sublimated into an essence: while on the other hand, many unnoticed Platonic ideas, relations, or unsubstantial aspects of things, when the thrill of beauty runs through them, are suddenly revealed, as in poetry the secret harmonies of feelings and of words. In this way innumerable natural themes of happiness,

Beauty detaches them for contemplation from the flux of nature.

which no one could possibly mistake for things, become members of the human family, and in turn restore the prodigal mind, perhaps long wasted on facts, to its home circle of essence.

This native affinity of the mind to essence rather than to fact is mind itself, the very nature of spirit or intellectual light. The sort of intelligence <sub>There is</sub> which adapts one natural being to another, <sub>concomitant</sub> and may be found in the conduct of animals, <sub>contemplation in the</sub> or even in the structure of their bodies, does <sub>midst of</sub> not consist in thinking; it is an adaptation <sub>action whenever</sub> of life to its conditions, a form of behaviour <sub>action is</sub> in matter, which must exist and flourish <sub>masterly.</sub> before thinking or even feeling can arise at all. Intuition would be impossible without an underlying animal life, a psyche; for how should the sheer light of intuition actualise itself, or choose the essence on which it should fall? A psyche, the hereditary organisation and movement of life in an animal, must first exist and sustain itself by its "intelligent" adaptations to the ambient world: but these adaptations are not conscious until, by virtue of their existence, intuition arises; and intuition arises when the inner life of the animal, or its contact with external things, is expressed in some actual appearance, in some essence given in feeling or thought. The psyche and the material circumstances, by their special character and movement, determine the choice and succession of themes on which intuition shall be employed in some particular person; in so far as spirit is kindled there at all, it will have raised those themes to the plane of essence; the whole movement of nature and of human affairs, which imposes those themes, becomes itself only another theme for contemplation, if present to the mind at all. This contemplation does not require a man to shut his eyes or to fix them exclusively on the stars; it does not require him to stop living or acting. Often the most contemplative

minds are the most worldly-wise, and the most capable
of directing business. But though they may survey or
foresee action, they do not live in action, because they
see it in its wholeness and in its results; as a spectator
who sees the plot of a play understands the emotions of
the characters; but does not succumb to them; or
as a writer, very busy with his pen and conveying much
ink from inkstand to paper, may be thinking of his
subject; and the words will probably come most aptly
when, as words, they come unconsciously, and when
the truth which they express absorbs the whole mind.
The same thing happens in a game of ball, or in the
game of politics, when the player is good; the quick
adjustment of his faculties and organs, being automatic,
kindles in his mind a graphic image and a pure
emotion, to be the signs of his achievement to his inner
man.

The natural and the spiritual fruits of life are not
opposed, but they are different. Its natural fruits are
Moral as     more life, persisting through readjustments
well as      and an incessant generation of new forms,
æsthetic
virtue is    so that youth may fill the place of age and
realised in  attain an equal, though not identical, perfec-
the con-
templation   tion. It is in these perfections, or in ap-
of essence.  proaches which partly anticipate them, that
the spiritual fruits are found. As we have seen,
they may ripen early, and may be gathered at all
seasons, when any phase of life is perfected in action;
but the spiritual fruits are internal or tangential to this
action, not consequent upon it, like the natural fruits:
they may be omnipresent in existence, but only by
everywhere transmuting existence into essence. Spirit
is life looking out of the window; the work of the
household must have been done first, and is best done
by machinery. Moral triumphs are not æsthetic,
because they have other occasions, but they are equally
intellectual when realised in the spirit; they lie in the

joy of having done *this*: they are a passage into essence. Finality, though it is not felt as beauty, marks the great moments of passion satisfied or purposes achieved. Into some scene, into some phrase, into some gesture in itself trivial, the whole burden of a long experience may then be cast, and happiness may be centred and realised in some simple event or in some silent moment.

I should need but to enlarge this canvass in order to paint the whole happiness possible to man. In what should it lie? In going on, and simply not stopping? In passing to some better experience? But in what would it be better? In being fuller or longer? I think the longer and the fuller a bad life is, the worse it is. How, then, should it be made better? Only surely, by bringing all its activities, as far as possible, to intrinsic perfection and mutual harmony, so that at each step, and in every high moment of synthesis and reflection, intuition may fall on an essence beyond which it need not look, finding in it peace, liberation, and a sufficient token that fate, so far as that expression of spirit is concerned, has lost its terrors. Without such vision realised at each of its stages, life would be a mere fatality, automatism at odds with itself, a procession of failures. Spirit would have been called into being by a false promise; its only hope would be that by sleep supervening, or by distraction so extreme as to destroy the organic harmonies on which intuition depends, that mistake should be corrected and forgotten.

This possible conflict between matter and spirit is a family quarrel; it is not a shock between independent forces brought together by accident, since spirit cannot exist except in matter, and matter cannot become interested in its formations and fortunes save by creating a spirit that may observe and celebrate them. How happily spirit and matter may lead their common

In normal life, as in play, intuition is the innocent expression of action.

life together appears in play at the beginning, and in contemplation at the end. It is only in the middle when animal faculties are inwardly perfect and keen enough to be conscious, but are outwardly ill-adjusted and ignorant, that trouble arises; because the mind sees and wants one thing, and circumstances impose something different, requiring a disposition and a form of imagination in the animal to which his play-life is not adapted. Spirit—the voice of the inner nature in so far as it is already formed and definite—accordingly suffers continual defeats, by the defeat of those animal impulses which it expresses; and if these impulses become confused or exhausted, it sinks with them into vice or discouragement. It would soon perish altogether, and annul the moral problem which its existence creates, unless in some way a harmony could be re-established between the individual and the world. This may be done in society at large by some firm political and moral regimen; or it may be done religiously by the discipline of the inner man, so that a part of him is weaned from the passions and interests which distract the world and is centred upon purely intellectual or spiritual aspiration. Religion is hard for external events to defeat, since ill-fortune stimulates it as much at least as good fortune. Thus within strict limits, and in a soberer garb, the play-life of childhood is restored to the soul.

Hence that happy quarrel of philosophers—happy because both parties are right—as to whether wisdom is a meditation on life or on death. But in the midst of one we are in the other, not only in that existence is transition, but far more remarkably, in that life triumphant is life transmuted into something which is not life—into union with essence, with so much of the eternal as is then manifested in the transitory. This manifestation, with all the approaches to it, is life itself;

*Life, death, and immortality all hang on the relation of existence to essence.*

and death is the fading of that vision, the passing of that essence back into its native heaven, depriving us by its obscuration of a part of ourselves, so that existence in us must lapse into some different phase, or into total darkness. Life, if by this word we understand the process of mutation, is itself death; to be fed is to kill, to advance is to reject and abandon. The truly creative movement is only upward, and life, in so far as it means light and accomplishment, is only some pre-destined intuition achieved, some wished-for essence made manifest. Existence itself is a momentary victory of essence : a victory over matter, in that matter, which might have taken any other form, takes this particular one and keeps circling about it, as if fascin-ated; not that there is really any magic here, but that matter, which has to have some form or other, is willing enough to be true to the one it has, and (so indifferent is it to form) to renounce for an indefinite time its native right to inconstancy : as a hardened traveller, not caring what inn he stays at, may remain good-naturedly at the one in which he happens to be lodged. Essence is victorious also over spirit, and no less amiably victorious; since it is in essence that spirit aspires to lose itself and to find its quietus, as it was from essence that matter managed to borrow some character and some beauty. What Spinoza meant by meditation on life was, I take it, the effort to wrest the truth of nature out of empirical confusion, so that all the vicissitudes of things might appear under the form of eternity; and what Socrates and Plato meant by meditation on death was almost the same thing. Only the Greeks, by distinguishing many gods and many divine ideas, could humanise and make friends with at least some of them; and in sympathy with those beautiful immortals they could survey and dismiss earthly existence with a touch of disdain; whereas the piety of thrifty and moralising nations, when enlightened,

issues only in a scrupulous natural philosophy.  Being
overawed by the facts, and eager for existence and
prosperity, they miss the liberal life;  they prefer
perpetual servitude, if well fed, to emancipation, such
as interest in pure essences affords;  and often (though
not in Spinoza) they substitute a troubled hope in some
fabulous resurrection for the present union with the
eternal which is natural to spirit.

Thus scepticism, dialectic, contemplation, and
spiritual discipline, all lead to the discrimination of

Essence,
to which
spirit is
addressed,
is not the
source of
spirit or
of any exist-
ing fact.

essence;  and anyone who has trodden any of
these paths to the end will not need to be told
what essence means, or that it is a most real
and interesting realm of being.  But it is not
the whole of being : on the contrary, were
there nothing but essence, not one of these
approaches to it would be open : there would
be no possible movement, no events, no life, and no
preference.  Considered in itself, essence is certainly
the deepest, the only inevitable, form of reality; but I
am here speaking of approaches to it, that is, of considerations drawn from human experience that may enable us
to discern that primary reality and to recognise it to be
such in contrast to our own form of being.  We stand,
then, on another plane, the plane of scattered experience, brute fact, contingent existence; if we did not,
the discernment of essence would have no novelty for
us, it would reveal no night-firmament behind our
day, it would not liberate us from ourselves or from the
incubus of accidental things.  If we were prompted,
then, by our new insight to cry that our old life was all
illusion, we might be turning this insight into a new
folly.  Enlightenment itself would be impossible if
chance experiences had not preceded, perfectly real in
their own way; indeed existence (something that has no
foothold whatever in the realm of essence) is presupposed and contained in any assertion or denial, and

in the intuition of essence itself. The existence and distribution of enlightenment, as of any other fact, places us to begin with in another realm, the realm of matter, which must be begged separately: without it there could be no manifestation of essence, whether in nature or in discourse.

The priority of the realm of essence is therefore not temporal or dynamic. It is an infinite field for selection; evidently it cannot select or em-phasise any part of itself. When the selection takes place, we accordingly refer it to a different principle, which we may call chance, fact, or matter: but this principle would be a mere word, a term without indicative force, if it did not select some feature of the realm of essence to be its chosen form: in other words, if this brute accident were not some accident in particular, contrasted with the infinity of other forms which it has not chosen. To appeal to fact, to thump existence with empirical con-viction, is accordingly but to emphasise some essence, like a virtuous bridegroom renouncing all others: the exclusion is opportune, but the bride after all is only one of a million, and the mind has simply wedded an essence. The principle of constancy, or perhaps of inconstancy—the selective principle—is matter; yet whatever way it may turn, it must embrace one essence or another.

*Matter is the selective principle even among essences.*

The approaches to essence are therefore as various as those predispositions in matter which deter-mine the poses of life. Or we may say that for the mind there is a single avenue to essence, namely, attention. Awaken attention, intensify it, purify it into white flame, and the actual and unsubstantial object of intuition will stand before you in all its living immediacy and innocent nakedness. But notice: this atten-tion, discovering nothing but essence, is itself an

*Through animal passions and interests, matter directs attention upon essence.*

animal faculty: it is called forth by material stress, or by passion. The passions, in so far as they are impulses to action, entangle us materially in the flux of substance, being intent on seizing, transforming, or destroying something that exists: but at the same time, in so far as they quicken the mind, they are favourable to the discernment of essence; and it is only a passionate soul that can be truly contemplative. The reward of the lover, which also chastens him, is to discover that in thinking he loved anything of this world he was profoundly mistaken. Everybody strives for possession; that is the animal instinct on which everything hangs; but possession leaves the true lover unsatisfied: his joy is in the character of the thing loved, in the essence it reveals, whether it be here or there, now or then, his or another's. This essence, which for action was only a signal letting loose a generic animal impulse, to contemplation is the whole object of love, and the sole gain in loving. Naturally essences seem thin abstractions to those absorbed in action, whose heart is set on the eventual, and to whom the actual is never anything: the actual in experience is never more than an echo or supplement to deeper facts, a shimmer on the surface of the great sea labouring beneath; yet the actual in experience is never an abstraction from experience itself; it is the whole fruit of that hidden labour, the entire reality for the spirit. It is therefore not as a quality attributed to external things that essence is best distinguished; for the colour or the shape of an apple may be supposed to exist in it, and when drawn out and imagined existing alone they may seem ghostly; neither the roundness nor the redness of the apple would be edible. To a greedy child they would be miserable cheats; but not so to the painter or the geometer. The child might be better initiated into the nature of essence (which is not far from the innocent mind) if he chose as an instance the pleasure of eating the apple, or of snatching it from another boy's hand; essences which he would distinguish easily from their opposites, and which he would not be tempted to incorporate into apples. A little experience would convince him that these intangible pleasures gave importance to apples, and not apples to them; and he would join the painter of still life, and the geometer, in finding that things are mere instruments, and that only essences are essential. Interest, in marking the differences and precise characters of things, which are all that the mind can take from them, is the great revealer of essence. Herein appears the thoroughly intellectual or poetical virtue of spirit. The more intense and dominating it is, the less it dwells on the machinery which may control its existence, and the more exclusively it addresses itself to the true or the beautiful, that is, to the essences which experience would manifest if it were pure and perfect.

# CHAPTER II

## THE BEING PROPER TO ESSENCES

THE principle of essence, we have seen, is identity: the being of each essence is entirely exhausted by its Each essence *is* by being identical and individual. definition; I do not mean its definition in words, but the character which distinguishes it from any other essence. Every essence is perfectly individual. There can be no question in the realm of essence of mistaken identity, vagueness, shiftiness, or self-contradiction. These doubts arise in respect to natural existences or the meanings or purposes of living minds : but in every doubt or equivocation both alternatives are genuine essences; and in groping and making up my mind I merely hesitate between essences, not knowing on which to arrest my attention. There is no possibility of flux or ambiguity within any of the alternatives which might be chosen at each step.

This inalienable individuality of each essence renders it a universal; for being perfectly self-contained Also universal. and real only by virtue of its intrinsic character, it contains no reference to any setting in space or time, and stands in no adventitious relations to anything. Therefore without forfeiting its absolute identity it may be repeated or reviewed any number of times. Such embodiments or views of it, like the copies of a book or the acts of reading of it, will be facts or events in nature (which is a net of external relations); but the copies would not be copies of the same book, nor the readings readings of it, unless (and in so far as) the same essence reappeared in them all. Physical obstacles to exact repetitions or reproductions do not affect the essential universality of every essence, even if by chance it occurs only once, or never occurs at all; because, in virtue of its perfect identity and individuality, it cannot fall out of the catalogue of essences, where it fills its particular place.   If I try to delete it, I reinstate it, since in deleting *that* I have recognised and defined it anew, bearing witness to its possessing the whole being which it can claim as an essence.   There accordingly it stands, waiting to be embodied or noticed, if nature or attention ever choose to halt at that point or to traverse it.   Every essence in its own realm is just as central, just as normal, and just as complete as any other : it is therefore always just as open to exemplification or to thought, without the addition or subtraction of one iota of its being. Time and space may claim and repeat it as often or as seldom as they will : that is their own affair.   The flux is free to have such plasticity as it has, and to miss all that it misses; and it is free to be as monotonous as it likes, if it finds it easier to fall again and again into the same form, rather than to run away into perpetual and unreturning novelties.   The realm of essence is the scale of measurement, the continuum of variation, on which these repetitions or these novelties may be plotted and compared.   Re-embodiments   or   re-surveys   of   an essence (if they occur) bind the parts of the flux together ideally, and render it amenable to description. The essential universality of these forms makes any fact, in so far as it exhibits them, distinct and knowable : the universal and the individual being so far from contrary that they are identical.   I am not myself unless I re-enact now the essence of myself, which I may re-enact at all times and places.

Since essences are universals not needing to figure in any particular place or time, but fit to figure in any, it is not possible to investigate the realm of essence by empirical exploration. You cannot go in search of that which is nowhere. Some essences will appear or occur to you, since whatever intuition life may awaken in you must light up some essence or other; but what further essences, if any, there may be is not discoverable by simply waiting for them to turn up. Nature is indeed very rich in forms, compared with the inertia and monotony of experience in home-keeping animals, revolving in their private circle of habits and ideas; but nature too is built on a single plan—all nuclei and planets, all life and death— and as much a slave of routine as any of her creatures. The unexemplified is not exemplified there, the unthought of is not thought of : not because in itself it resists being created or described, but because nature and thought happen not to bloom in any way but that in which they have taken to blooming. In part, indeed, this restriction may be due to local prejudice and ignorance in the observer, who draws the periphery of nature with his compass. Another man, a different animal, a spirit native to another world may even now be greeting the essences which it has not entered into my heart to conceive. Evidently my limitations cannot forbid them to rejoice in their different experience; nor can the limitations of any actual experience forbid the essences it leaves out to be just those which are absent. An essence is an inert theme, something which cannot bring itself forward, but must be chosen, if chosen, by some external agent; and evidently the choice made by this agent, contingent as it is and wholly arbitrary, cannot render unavailable the other inert themes which other agents, or itself in a different moment of its flux, might choose instead. The very contingency of existence, the very blindness of life,

*Essences are infinite in number.*

THE BEING PROPER TO ESSENCES

throw the doors wide open towards the infinity of being. Even if some philosopher or some god thought himself omniscient, surprises might be in store for him, and thoughts new to his thought; nay, even supposing that his whole experience and the entire history of his world lay synthesised before him under the form of eternity, and that he was not a victim of sheer egotism in asserting that nothing more could ever exist, still the wanton idiosyncrasy of that total fact, the enormity of that accident, could not be blustered away. Existence is irrational for a deeper and more intrinsic reason than because one part of it may not be deducible from another : any part, and all its parts together, are irrational in merely existing, and in being otherwise than as essences are, that is, identical with themselves and endowed with that formal being which it is impossible that anything, whatever it be, should not possess. Not that essence can resist or resent this irrational selection which existence makes of its riches: on the contrary, essence is a sort of invitation to the dance; it tempts nature with openings in every direction ; and in so doing it manifests its own inexhaustible variety. Its very being is to set no limits to the forms of being. The multitude of essences is absolutely infinite.

This assertion has an audacious sound, and I should not venture upon it, had it not a counterpart or corollary which takes away all its venom, namely, that But non-essences do not *exist*. If I were in pursuit of existent; substance (as I shall be in the Second Book) they form I should distrust any description of it not an indelible purely tentative, empirical, and scrupulously background modest: but the bold definition which Spinoza facts. gives of what he calls substance that it is Being absolutely infinite, seems to me a perfect and self-justifying definition of the realm of essence: because in conceiving and defining such an object we prove it to possess the only being which we mean to ascribe to it. Denying it to be infinite, or denying that any supposed element in it existed, we should be designating these missing elements and that absent infinity: whereby we should be instituting them ideally, and recognising them to be essences. The realm of essence is comparable to an infinite Koran—or the Logos that was in the beginning—written in invisible but indelible ink, prophesying all that Being could ever be or contain: and the flux of existence is the magical re-agent, travelling over it in a thin stream, like a reader's eye, and bringing here one snatch of it and there another to the light for a passing moment. Each reader may be satisfied with his own verse, and think it the whole of Scripture: but the mere assertion of this limit, or suspicion that other readers might find other texts, is enough to show that the non-existent cannot be limited, since the limits of the existent might always be changed. To deny the being of essence, because it may happen to be unrealised, is self-contradictory: for if it is not realised, it must have a quality, distinguishing it from realised forms. Unrealised forms may not interest a sluggish mind: an arithmetician who was happy in the thought of whole numbers, might deprecate all mention of vulgar fractions or repeating decimals, and might swear to die without them, lest his safe and honest arithmetic should be complicated with unrealities. But unrealities of that sort nevertheless envelop his realities on every side; and it is his arrest at his realities that, if you like, is unreal; there is no reason in it, and no permanence; whereas the unrealities are unchangeable, inevitable, and always standing behind the door. Even if the whole realm of essence (as Spinoza assumed) were realised somewhere at some time in the life of nature, essence would remain a different and a non-existent realm: because the realisation of each part

could be only local and temporary, and for all the rest
of time and in all the worlds that excluded it, each fact
would fade into the corresponding essence, and would
remain certain and inevitable as an essence only, and as
a fact merely presumptive.

Essence so understood much more truly *is* than any
substance or any experience or any event: for a substance, event, or experience may change its    Existence
form or may exist only by changing it, so that  and truth
all sorts of things that are proper to it in one  borrow their
                                                  individuality
phase will be absent from it in another.   It  from essence.
will not be a unit at all, save by external delimitation.
Perhaps some abstract constancy in quantity, energy,
or continuity may be discovered to run through it, but
this constant element will never be the actual experience, event, or substance in its living totality at any
moment.   Or perhaps all the phases of such an existence may be viewed together and synthesised into one
historical picture; but this picture would again not be
the existent substance, experience, or event unrolling
itself in act.   It would be only a description of that
portion of the flux seen under the form of eternity;
in other words, it would be an essence and not an
existence.   Essence is just that character which any
existence wears in so far as it remains identical with
itself and so long as it does so; the very character which
it throws overboard by changing, and loses altogether
when it becomes something else.   To be able to
become something else, to suffer change and yet endure,
is the privilege of existence, be it in a substance, an
event, or an experience; whereas essences can be exchanged, but not changed.   Existence at every step
casts off one essence and picks up another: we call it
the same existence when we are able to trace its continuity in change, by virtue of its locus and proportions;
but often we are constrained to give up the count, and
to speak of a new event, a new thing, or a new experi-

ence. The essences or forms traversed in mutation
render this mutation possible and describable: without their eternal distinctness no part of the flux could
differ in any respect from any other part, and the whole
would collapse into a lump without order or quality.
So much more profound is the eternal being of the
essences traversed in change, than that of the matter
or attention or discourse which plays with those
essences at touch and go.

Nothing, then, more truly *is* than character. Without this wedding garment no guest is admitted to the
Notion of feast of existence: whereas the unbidden
the Realm essences do not require that invitation (with
of Essence. which very low characters are sometimes
honoured) in order to preserve their proud identity
out in the cold. There those few privileged revellers
will soon have to rejoin them, not a whit fatter for their
brief surfeit of being. After things lose their existence,
as before they attain it, although it is true of them that
they have existed or will exist, they have no internal
being except their essences, quite as if they had never
broached Existence at all: yet the identity of each
essence with itself and difference from every other
essence suffices to distinguish and define them all in
eternity, where they form the Realm of Essence. True
and false assertions may be made about any one of
them, such, for instance, as that it does not exist; or
that it includes or excludes some other essence, or is
included or excluded by it.

Here is a further character inseparable from essence:
all essences are eternal. No hyperbole or rhetorical
Its eternity afflatus is contained in this assertion, as if
is the some prophet pronounced some law or some
counterpart city to be everlasting. That any existing
of its non-
existence. thing should be everlasting, though not
impossible, is incongruous with the contingency of
existence. God or matter, if they are everlasting, are

so by a sort of iterated contingency and perpetual reproduction; for it is in the nature of existence to be here and perhaps not there, now and perhaps not then; it must be explored to discover how far it may stretch; it must wait and see how long it shall last. The assumption that it lasts or stretches for ever can be made only impetuously, by animal enthusiasm, when the feeling of readiness and omnipotence makes some living creature defy all threats of disaster. Yet so long as we live in time, the ghost of the murdered past will always fill the present with a profound uneasiness. If the eternity of essence were conceived after that fashion, it would indeed be a rash boast; no essence has an essential lien on existence anywhere, much less everywhere and always. Its eternity has nothing to do with such mortal hazards. It is merely the self-identity proper to each of the forms which existence may put on or off, illustrate somewhere or perhaps illustrate always, or very likely never illustrate at all.

# CHAPTER III

## ADVENTITIOUS ASPECTS OF ESSENCE

THE realm of essence, like the empyrean, is a clear and tranquil region when you once reach it; but for the observer from the earth clouds may inter-

*In many impure speculative terms essence is fused with existence.*

vene, or his eye may be arrested at some nearer sphere which, just because it has some opaqueness, he may think the true blue. Instead of conceiving essences he may conceive possible beings, problematical facts, forms of things, abstractions, thoughts, sensations, or natural elements. Of course such intermediate objects, however they be defined, will exhibit some essence, since some essence cannot help appearing in any chosen thing whatsoever; but in the categories just mentioned there is some ambiguity, some reference to contingent existence, which limits their scope, and renders them altogether confusing, if taken as synonyms for essential being.

The word " possible " is slippery and treacherous. It is commonly applied to anything that the speaker

*Essence not possible being.*

can readily imagine, especially when he is ignorant whether it is a fact or not. In this sense the whole future, and much of the past, is called possible when imaginable. But in another sense the whole past and future, even when unimaginable, must have been possible too. The materially possible threatens to coincide with the actual course

26

of nature: and then the term possible begins to mean
the materially impossible, provided it is imaginable.
The imagination, however, is itself something existent,
and extremely elastic: a little shake, or a new stimulus,
will cause it to conceive many new possibilities. Can
these have been impossibilities before? Perhaps we
may take refuge in the notion that everything is possible
except what is self-contradictory: in other words,
things are not possible merely because they are actual,
or merely because they are imagined, but if they are
such as not to preclude being imagined. But how
should anything preclude being imagined, if an imagination arose capable of imagining it? The meaning
can only be that my own imagination, in some particular instance, has got into a tangle, and that in
speaking of the round square or of the son of a barren
woman I have lost the meaning of my terms; and
what I call an impossibility is only the suspense of
my thought between two possibilities. Nothing contradicts itself, not even this state of confusion in
my thinking. It is a perfectly possible muddle. This
process of fluctuating from one object to another has a
character easily recognisable; its essence, like every
essence, is individual and (since it may reappear) is
universal. Contradiction is a vice into which discourse may fall when it blurs the inherent distinctness
of different essences. Determination, individuality,
variety infinitely precise and indelible (degrees of
articulation being themselves all equally distinct) is
the very being of essence. Howsoever monistic
physics may choose to be, the realm of essence is the
home of eternal and irreducible plurality.

The terms " possible " and " impossible " have, then,
no proper application in the realm of essence; even
to facts in nature they are applicable only in view of
human ignorance or imagination. Their true field
is that of discourse, where the intent to consider one

essence binds the mind to fidelity and consistency, and excludes the substitution of another essence under the same name—excludes it, I mean, if the intent is maintained to express the essence originally chosen.  Hence the extension of the "possible" and the "impossible" to natural facts, in so far as their names or relations are assumed to prejudge their character: in a given world, describable by a given essence, anything contrary to that essence is impossible.  In the actual universe, its essence being completely determined by the events which compose it, all that is actual is necessary and all else is impossible.  But this of course does not preclude the possibility of any different world; and so long as the complete essence of the actual universe is unknown to us, we may give its name to almost any extensions or transformations of the part which we presume to know: so that the known world will be free to become, or to have been, almost anything.

*Nothing impossible, except that one essence should be another.*

The contingency of existence, though intrinsic to it, and the hypothetical nature of all reasoning about it, are a trial to logicians: they would like their art to rule *a priori*.  Many of them, in their eagerness to make logic dominant, betray it, by reducing it to a description of what they presume to be the natural movement of thought or of history: but there are some too devoted and clear-headed for such a subterfuge, who nevertheless wish to chain existence to their chariot.  How do so?  I know only of one way: to assert that the whole realm of essence is realised in existence.  The existence of an infinity of worlds irrelevant to ours, and utterly undiscoverable by us, cannot be precluded by our ignorance of them: the supposition is merely idle.  But another consequence involved in this hypothesis is positively repugnant to common sense; and this is, that an infinity of worlds almost identical with ours,

*Natural necessity is not logical.*

but differing from it in some detail, must exist too. An infinite number of solar systems, for instance, must have begun as ours began, but each of them must have deviated at one point from ours in its evolution, all the previous incidents being followed, in each case, by a different sequel. The interest in natural derivation which animates the observant and artful mind is thus outraged by the demand for logical completeness in things: and there can be little doubt to which side the sense for fact, which alone can judge of facts, will incline the naturalist.

By a somewhat different opposition to accidental facts, essence might be called "the imaginary". This designation is popular and poetically very appropriate, since the realm of essence is unsubstantial, remote from existence, and in- finitely more extensive. In broaching it we escape the limitations of fortune, as the poet does in his fictions; and yet the objects that greet us there may be more definite, memorable, and beautiful than the sordid facts, which we live among without feeling for them, perhaps, any intellectual affinity. But the danger in calling essence imaginary is that, like poetry, we should identify it with the imagined. The imagined is indeed unsubstantial, but it is selected, insecure, and de- pendent for its specious actuality on the vapours of some animal psyche. The imagined is not, as essence is, a field from which all facts must gather their tem- porary forms; it is only a replica or variant of some of these facts — namely, of human sensations — richer perhaps in spots than material reality, but on the whole far thinner and less extensive. Images drifting through idle heads are in their psychological dimension a part of the actual, since the intuition of those imaginary objects occurs at definite times and places. The im- aginary, if it is to mean essence, is the infinite fairy- land of which such dreams are glimpses. The moral

*Essences are not the imaginary.*

connotation of the word imaginary is also ambiguous. Actual images, being generated in the living psyche, may be very apposite fulfilments to her previous experience or to her instinctive needs, and therefore very beautiful; and actual dreams, even if for the most part silly and fatiguing, are sometimes pleasant and even prophetic. Nothing of the sort can be said of the imaginary as a whole, conceived as the realm of essence. Not being selected or produced by any living soul, but inert, infinite, and latent, it contains an appalling multitude of vain and ugly themes, as well as the few which are relevant to human interests and fit for human contemplation.

If free imagination presents stray essences to the mind, attentive perception presents others, to which studious people give greater importance. The flux of nature could not be a flux, nor at all perceptible, unless it was a flux through essences, that is, through forms of being differing from one another. It is as the forms things wear to the senses or to the practised intellect that essences are first noticed; in this capacity, or as definitions of current terms, they appear in the Socratic school. Geometrical figures, fixed by intent, are certainly essences; so too are any types of animal bodies or human institutions which may be arrested in thought : but so also are all the qualities of sensation despised by Platonism and all the types of change or relation neglected by that philosophy. This neglect was ominous, because if essences had been studied for their own sake they would have been found everywhere, as they are by the poet or the mathematician. To discern them only in natural or moral units, and to think of them as perfections towards which things aspire, is not merely to omit noticing them elsewhere but to regard them as natural magnets, as a background of metaphysical powers, more selective than nature itself, and

Nor the forms of things.

constituting a world of substances behind the flux of appearance. Physics and theology may appeal to such patron substances if they think fit; but in the theory of essence they have no place whatever. Essences are not substances containing a matter that can assume a different essence : they cannot be the material source of anything. Nor have they any relevance to particular places and times, so that one might be conceived to preside over one part of nature, and another over another. The essence of a bridge cannot build bridges or breed them; and when a bridge falls and the matter of it becomes a heap of stones, the essence of that bridge is not a surviving ghost haunting the spot, and seeking to restore the structure. A material bridge-builder must return to the work: and the resulting form will hardly repeat exactly the one that has disappeared; nor will that discarded essence fight against reform, or in any way complain or avenge itself, if presently bridge-builders come no more to the spot, and the placid stream flows on unspanned, reflecting no shadow of any human contrivance. So it is also, in spite of superstition, with the essences of living beings, which reproduce themselves for generations with little change of type. Their conservation is physical and an elaborate instance of rhythm and habit in matter. Here too a material seed must transmit the substance that is to run through the ancestral cycle and embody that familiar essence: let the seed fail, or circumstances modify it, and at once that prescribed form is forsaken and forgotten, relegated to the realm of essence and reduced to the same impotence, or left in the same peace, as all its sister essences that time has never brought to existence.

The most stubborn misunderstanding of essence arises, however, from thinking and calling it an abstraction. In a popular sense the epithet is natural and harmless: it means only that essence is immaterial.

So mathematics is called an abstract science and music
an abstract art; they do not describe particular parts
of the material world or particular historical
events; they may therefore seem unreal and
superfluous to the man in the street.   But
the mathematician or the musician will hardly
call them *abstract*, since his apprehension
of them is direct and his interest in them
primary.   No doubt the material world, especially
in his own person and life, supplies a suggestion and an
organ for those intuitions; but their object is so far
from being drawn out of existing things that it never
exists in them in its ideal perfection, and the study of
it requires a special imaginative faculty, a profound
application, and a great exactitude.   It is the very
complexity and precise definition of this realm—its
essential concreteness—that renders it difficult and
vague to the gross mind: and it is called abstract not
because it is drawn from existence but because it is not
found there.

Nor abstrac-
tions.   The
immaterial
is not
abstracted
from the
material.

It is an accident to essence to be manifested; but
not to be manifested is also an accident; it means
simply that matter or intellect happen never to have
traversed that form.   A different plasticity in existence
might make any essence an appearance; and evidently
in a given appearance there can be nothing abstract—
nothing verbal, unrealisable, or cognitively secondary.
Each appearance (and therefore every essence, since
it might well appear) is an obvious and complete being;
and if essences when simple are indefinable, that fact
only proves that they are the original elements of any
description.   Far from being creatures of language,
they suffer from not being commonly named, since
names are hurriedly clapped on things and persons,
however ill perceived, which move as material units;
whereas the most evident features in immediate
experience receive no separate names, until perhaps

some logician, poet, or madman grows conscious of their perpetual presence, and borrows some title for them from the vocabulary of physics; as I have borrowed this term "essence," once used by chemists for their drugs, in order to designate every specious object actually present to intuition. Language is responsible, not for these objects, but for the prejudice against them. An essence, if un-named, is thought to be imperfect and but half real. An unchristened child has to be called So-and-So's baby, and a stranger in the street has to be pointed at dumbly; yet it would be too egotistical even for human nature to assert that the waif or the stranger possessed no being of his own, but was essentially an abstraction from our social circle, because he could be described in our language only relatively and peripherally. It is not otherwise with the immediate, radical, nameless phantoms of feeling and intuition. They are just the appearances they are, exactly determinate and perfect at each moment, and different in some precise way from whatever else may be felt before or after or by other people; and the necessary defects, or rather the proper summary function, of language or reflection, must not be charged against those primary appearances as a defect of essence.

When a term is felt to be disparaging, as the term abstract has become for some writers, it can easily be passed on from one bad thing to another. Instead of designating defect of form abstract-ness may designate defect of quantity. In an etymological sense any part of a thing, like the skin of an apple when peeled off, might be called an abstraction from the whole, especially when the part abstracted happens not to have existed separately in the beginning, *If the parts, when de-tached from a whole, be called abstractions, all things are abstrac-tions from the realm of essence.* as do the bricks of a house, but to have grown up together with the whole, and been first found there. Hence a well-known doctrine that only the Absolute is concrete

D

and that every particular fact or observation is an abstraction. In this sense of the word, every essence would be an abstraction from the realm of essence, but no essence, much less the realm of essence in its entirety, would be an abstraction from existing things: on the contrary, existing things would be abstractions from their essences, which in the realm of essence possess much richer essential relations than those which in existing instances are abstracted and realised materially. The rind of the apple, peeled and curling casually on a plate, would be a miserable abstraction from all the spirals and all the patterns implied in its geometrical essence and in its pictorial aspect.

Abstraction, however, in the proper sense of the word, is possible only for a mind: things and essences, whatever may be their unions or separations, are never in their own being abstractions from anything else. A term can be abstract only relatively: how should anything be abstract in itself? None of the constituents of a thing or of an essence is an abstraction from it; each is a thing or an essence in its own right. To find abstractions we must enter the psychological sphere and consider the casual history of human ideas. A late idea, though its object may be perfectly concrete and definite, like the sphere, may be simple in comparison with some early impression—say, that of an apple—which may have first suggested it: and if the variegated essence was really distinguished first (which is not always the case) and the simple one —roundness—was only noticed afterwards as an element included in the other, then, for that person the sphere will be something abstract, not indeed in its essence, but in its mode of reaching manifestation: an act of abstraction happens first to have revealed this essence to this man. But such an approach is accidental: a true psychologist would often record that in

*Abstraction is an operation in discourse, relative, adventitious, and alien to the essences concerned.*

looking at some roundish thing he first noticed and intuited nothing but roundness, perfect, Platonic, and unadulterated. The clumsiest spheroid cannot convey to an innocent mind any idea save that of a simple sphere; and our first impression of a world in which everything is crooked is that everything is straight. The enormity of our childish idealism would prove immediately fatal if we needed to have a true idea of things in order to act properly in their presence. But ideas which are ridiculous as descriptions may be adequate as signals: all animals eat and breed without any notion of calorics or eugenics: hunger and love are moral overtones quite sufficient to express for them their share in the rude economy of nature. The mind is not a fifth wheel to her coach, but her observations on the journey. Conventional psychology is misled by a primitive gnostic theory to the effect that things ought normally to appear to sense in their full and exact nature. Nothing could be further from the fact, or more incongruous with animal life and sensibility. That which appears to sense is determined at each moment by the liveliness and direction of the psyche in her current reactions. Things are thereby " known " in the sense that they are named, and distinguished by their rough aspect and occasions; they are not known at all in the sense of being disclosed in their inner nature, either totally or partially. The specious essence intuited is the *name* given by the psyche to the material force encountered or exerted; it is a spontaneous symbol, not abstract even in its origin; as the word cat is not drawn out of the domestic animal, yet serves to designate it in its entirety, and is much simpler.

Repetition is impossible in the realm of essence; two essences, if not different, will be one essence; if different they will be two essences, and not repetitions of the same essence. Repetition is possible only among objects which are particular but not individual; that is, when they exist and are distinguished by their external relations, even if internally they should happen Essences not general terms. to be precisely similar, and should have but one individuality or essence. An individual may change his relations and have different moments and places of existence, so that here he may be surrounded by one environment and there by another. This possibility of iterating or repeating an essence is what, from the point of view of existence, makes essences seem abstract or general, when in reality they are the only individuals. An essence is not the thing which it defines, and may define many things numerically distinct: what is ordinarily called one thing or one person has many separable moments of existence, between any two of which it may perish: they will be moments of one thing or one person only in so far as one individual essence pervades those moments. As nothing can be abstract in itself, so nothing can be general in itself. Every essence is universal not because there are repeated manifestations of it (for there need be no manifestations at all) but because it is individuated internally by its character, not externally by its position in the flux of nature: and no essence is general for the same reason. However it may be related to particular existences, its own nature is complete and intrinsic; whereas a term can be said to be general only if it happens to be predicable of a number of scattered things, none of which, perhaps, it defines intrinsically. Yet everything that is at all must be something intrinsically: had a term no individual essence there would be no meaning in predicating it, and it could not be predicated of two things in the same sense, since it would have no sense. Before essences can be called—occasionally and in relation to natural things—either abstract or general, it is requisite that in themselves they should be concrete and individual.

The organ of intuition is an animal psyche, governed by the laws of material life, in other words, by habit: so that it is normal for intuitions to be recur- rent, in so far as circumstances allow. Dis- course, in which intuitions subserve intent, requires intended essences to recur identically, and imputes identity to them even when they are different, if their difference is irrelevant to the cogency of discourse, and incom- patible with it. It is these intended essences, identical for intent on various occasions, but never actually intuited, that might well be called abstractions: they are like points of the compass, or limits of un-ending approaches, ideal in the sense of being never realised, although clearly indicated and definable by their relation to other terms which are actually given. The identity of an essence with itself is absolute and constitutional, but the identity of the essence given in one intuition with that given in another is an identity assumed and always unverifiable. It is impossible to arrest the two intuitions and compare their objects: to do this would be to supersede both by a third in which perhaps twin objects were presented: but it would remain an assumption that one twin repeated the datum of one intuition, and the other twin the datum of the other. Yet the impetuosity of life, which dis-course cannot help sharing, brushes aside these scruples: habit—iteration of words, gestures, and sentiments—sufficiently identifies the essence meant at one moment with that meant at another, in contempt of the varying context in which they may appear. This essence, not the context, is probably the only object distinctly noticed, or designated expressly. Thus the essence of straightness is continually intuited afresh, and is absolutely identical at each recurrence. It is irrelevant that the material object evoking this essence may be different in each instance, and never quite straight:

that context, even if vaguely pressing on the psyche, remains unsynthesised, unnoticed, and unintended. When on looking at a palm tree, a Roman road, or the horizon, I say to myself, How straight! I have exactly the same clear feeling: and this pure essence, not its irrelevant context, is what actually fills my mind, and is the essence apprehended. All the concomitant stuff, if it were noticed in turn, would merely supply other essences of the same universality. It is impossible that anything should appear which is not universal: for it is definite and might evidently appear again. Hence the possibility of discourse: its terms are coined into fixed values, and can pass from mind to mind, retaining their original meaning.

But mind is not a subject congenial to psychologists: they would like it either to reproduce material facts or to take its place among them, or even to swallow them up and be another name for them. Since the edges of material things are known to be broken and warped in fact, it is presumed that we must actually see all lines curved or broken. But mind is intrinsically and initially mind: it is poetical and Platonic from the beginning; and it is only by a painful eventual reinspection that it can correct its first impressions and allow that material things have in fact forms too complicated for the eye to trace, and a substance too remote in its pregnant texture from the scale of sense to be easily imagined, or to be imaginable by man at all. All this subterranean obscurity, however, is in its place: a wise man will not repine at it. Where clearness belongs, clearness enough may be found: the essences actually defined by attention are plain, brilliant, and homely, like the words of the vernacular. The psyche, a plodding beast, needs but to fall into her old paces for the old visions to reappear. It is essences, not things, that are on the human scale—

*Living mind, which is intellect in act, ignored by psychology.*

not all essences, of course, but those which the mind evokes spontaneously : whereas things, if humanised at all, can be humanised only by a long architectural labour —a labour which their insidious lapse very soon defeats and annuls.

That essences, though universals, are individual and are given bodily in intuition, may be better understood if we consider those existing things which are supposed to be concrete in contrast to essences. Their existence, we shall find, depends on their external relations, on their inclusion in the flux of nature; and science, in proportion as it penetrates to their dynamic structure and movement, becomes more and more mathematical, that is, operates with categories and terms more and more remote from pictorial physics. It is only when some portion of this inconceivably rapid and complicated flux of matter becomes recognisable and traceable in some respect, that a somewhat concrete thing can be found to exist. In other words, the concreteness of things is borrowed from the presence in them of some essence supposed to be abstract. Only when the flux, by its concentrations and sustained rhythms, manifests for a while locally some recognisable identity of form, can we speak of a concretion in existence, that is, of a thing. Abandon that essence, and that thing has dissolved. Certainly this essence, if it is to qualify existence, must be manifested or embodied in some nexus of events, amid variable external relations; but the flux of events itself would be the most empty of unrealities if it still pretended to flow after having obliterated within itself all distinctions of quality, direction, or phase—that is, all self-identical essences. Essences are definite and thinkable : existence is indefinite and only endured. That is the Platonic experience which I cannot help repeating and confirming at every turn; only that by

*Things and facts are essences sustained in the flux of nature.*

"thinkable" we must not understand definable in words, but open to intuition in the terms of any sense or of any logic. The flux flows by flowing through essences; and essences are manifested as the flux of matter or of attention picks them up and drops them.

An essence, then, is no abstraction, no unrealisable generality, but any actual aspect which anything can wear, determining its nature, or revealing it to an attentive mind. The sweetness I may taste is not dependent in the order of knowledge or of being upon abstraction from anything else. In my experience it is very likely the first indication I have of any substance called sugar existing near me, to be appropriated or investigated further. When I have gathered all I can learn about sugar, the sweetness originally tasted cannot become an abstraction from this much more remote and hypothetical object. It remains a self-sufficient essence, perhaps the only one given at the moment; but its appearance has now become, for my discursive thinking and belief, a symptom of certain chemical facts in the posited material world which I believe myself to inhabit.

Objects, whether essences or facts, may be considered recurrently, on separate occasions and by separate minds: otherwise discourse and experience could have no sanity, and could accumulate knowledge on no subject. On each occasion, however, the intuition, sensation, or thought turned upon that object is a fresh event, not only numerically but almost certainly by virtue of variations in its quality, context, and mental fringe; so that the living feeling or experience of the moment is something in flux, unseizable, not recoverable, and never, even when it existed, brought under the unity of apperception. Experience is something that just because it exists (without rising to the actuality of spirit) never exists all at once as a unit but only by

*Essences not active ideas, sensations, or thoughts.*

virtue of its parts, its movement, and its stress. Its parts exist, as it does itself, by occurring in a system of changes and conjunctions never given in such fleeting intuitions as it may include, and probably never given in intuition at all, even in the most accurate retrospect; because these moving clouds of sensibility and intent— the waking dreams of the psyche—are not objects which human attention is fitted or required to apprehend; they are complexes of no stability or importance as units; nothing matters in them save the objects discerned by them, or discerned by us afterwards as the goals of their movement. In discerning any of these objects, whether they be essences or things, animal life becomes intuition, the synthesis of attention by which an essence appears; but this intellectual act is wholly focussed on its object and unified only there. Taken as tension or potential perception, sensibility is diffused through indefinite time and through many vital functions; it would never exist actually and become a sensation unless it became the sensation of something; the intuition of some essence, like a pain or a sound.

An essence is, then, not at all a mental state, a sensation, perception, or living thought; it is not an "idea", as this word is understood in British philosophy. It is an "idea" only in the Platonic or graphic sense of being a theme open to consideration. Mental facts are not units either in nature or in logic; they are sub-divisions made by literary psychologists in the flux of experience considered romantically, as a biography abstracted from its organs and from its natural setting. The dream of life exists: it is going on perpetually in each of us; but its parts, called feelings and thoughts, are individuated only by the essences they discern, which are not the essences of those feelings or thoughts taken existentially, as moments in a dream, but are the essences of anything and everything under heaven or over it. If I think of God, the essence before me, my passing notion of the divine nature, individuates that thought of mine, and makes it possible for discourse afterwards to attribute it to me; but my thought was not God as it conceived God; it was a wretched mixture of words, memories, and dialectical gropings in my heated brain. So far is an existing idea from being the essence which it conceives.

If a romantic psychologist ever succeeded in reconstructing a moment of mental life exactly as it existed, he would be reconstructing (in the fresh setting of his own thoughts) an event itself perfectly particular and never destined to recur. But evidently, since his reconstruction is accurate, the essence given in that past moment is given again to him now; and it must recur in so far as any historian afterwards conceives that experience truly. The repetition of events is impossible, the recovery of essences is easy. Many a dead man, for instance, has considered the dyad in the form of twins, two shillings, or the numeral 2; and twins, two shillings, and the numeral 2 are still found in the world. This dyad, though I give it a learned name, is, indeed, the burden of a primitive intuition. The cat has it when she misses one of her two kittens, and the foreigner conveys it by holding up two fingers: it is not the fingers or the absent kitten that then absorb attention, but the instantly felt difference between one and two. In the midst of various vague and unsteady fields of experience quick intuition continually recovers this important primary essence. Hugging it, the mind can fly from world to world, and can make something definite and concrete out of their chaos, in so far as the dyad finds application there.

Animals live huddled among things and necessarily watchful of them, except in those hours of stolid composure in which they seem to be contemptuously

Mental events are particular and indefinable: essences are obvious and universal.

availing themselves of the chance not to think; whenever they think, however, whether in dreams or in action,
they can think only in terms of essences: and Finally,
hence that fundamental illusion, that hypo- essences
stasis of given essences, which the philosopher are not
should regard as normal and amiable, while parts of
avoiding it in his own person as far as things.
possible. He will succeed in this self-discipline in
proportion as his interests are intellectual and set
on essences rather than on things; he will then
feel the sharp contrast between the clear hypothetical
pictures in his thoughts and the dark complexities of
nature: he will be constantly aware of being an im-
pressionist in physics, a dramatist in psychology, a
novelist in history, and a pure dialectician in mathematics. But other philosophers are not lacking to
defend the illusion which animal faith imposes on
everybody until criticism comes to distinguish the
sphere of action from the language in which imagination expresses its adventures there. When intuition
remains closely attached to urgent action—in hunting,
for instance, or in pain—the essences appearing seem
actually to inhabit the material object or the bodily
member into which perception projects them. Given
essences then seem to be constituents of substances,
even when they are descriptive of perfectly immaterial
facts, like intentions and feelings: such sentiments, as
imagined by the observer, are boldly attributed to
other people, and thought of as agencies at work within
them. This dramatic sort of hypostasis is after all the
most defensible, because if the observer and the
observed are similar creatures in similar circumstances,
they will really be having similar intuitions; so that
our wild shot will hit the bull's eye by a pre-established
harmony. The transcript of nature in discourse will,
of course, remain poetical, since a man's sentiments are
but unrhymed poems which nature improvises within

him; but one poet may truly understand and repeat another.

It is harder to conceive how the form of a hollow sphere and the colour blue can help to compose the substance of aerial space, or where exactly they shall be deputed to lodge: nor is it clear how these essences can occupy some nearer locus, such as a nerve or a brain. It will not help to call these appearances qualities of things, rather than parts, if the qualities are supposed to be intrinsic: the intrinsic qualities of a thing compose its essence, and its essence, when caught in external relations, is the thing itself. If on the contrary by calling appearances qualities rather than parts of things, it be meant that these qualities are adventitious and relative, the contention is valid; because any aspect, effect, or relation accruing to a thing justifies a new epithet being assigned to it, as on my birth a whole series of dead men, up to Adam, suddenly became my ancestors. So when a human eye is turned skyward, the sky truly acquires the quality of looking blue and round: those are its real qualities in relation to such an observer, as certain substances are truly poison for rats.

These ulterior questions, however, cannot arrest the impetuous dogmatic instinct which asserts things to be what they seem and to exist in the very terms in which they appear. The stones would laugh, if they got wind of this human assurance; but meantime it is not useless in developing human acquaintance with essences: because this incongruous dignity attributed to them, of being material things, has the merit of attaching practical minds to them; and later, if these wise men discover their error, they may have acquired the habit of defining essences, and may find them worth cleaving to for their own sake.

*But appearances, which are essences, are the qualities of things for experience.*

# CHAPTER IV

## PURE BEING

OF all essences the most lauded and the most despised,
the most intently studied in some quarters and the
most misunderstood in others, is pure Being.  Confusions
It has been identified with nothing, with about pure
matter, and with God; and even among those  Being.
who regard it in its logical purity, it is sometimes said
to be the richest and most comprehensive of essences
and sometimes the poorest and most abstract.

No essence, as we have seen, is abstract essentially,
since it defines itself and might appear alone to an
intellect strung to that key: and in the case of pure
Being we have high testimony (which there is no reason
to distrust) assuring us that, in fact, it appears alone to
the human intellect in its ultimate reaches; and even
when not realised separately in intuition, it can be
discerned both analytically and intuitively in every
essence whatsoever.  Pure Being supplies, as it were,
the logical or æsthetic matter which all essences have
in common, and which reduces them to comparable
modes on one plane of reality.  Pure Being is thus
found in all essences somewhat as light is in all colours
or life in all feeling and thought; and philosophers like
Parmenides and Spinoza (not to speak here of the
Indians) assure us that we always have an adequate
intuition of this pure Being, usually buried under vain
illusions, but when unearthed and isolated seen to be

very mighty in itself and easily recognisable. Nevertheless such assurances may mean little to other mortals. Language at these depths of attentiveness is perforce the language of solitaries. When repeated it may not carry with it the intuition which it was first meant to record. The very logicians who distinguish this essence, because they call it Being, may conclude that nothing else can *be*—a most perplexing inference and, in view of the many meanings of the word *is*, a most misleading one; while other logicians, because pure Being is different from all other essences, may hastily identify it with nothing, by a strange equivocation between nothing and nothing else.

Confusion in this matter comes chiefly from the equivocation between being and existence. Initially this equivocation is normal, innocent, and even expedient, like any substitution of names for things: it is only when defended theoretically that it becomes perverse. Intelligence begins with it: animals are surrounded by things that affect their condition and prompt their reactions, so that their attention is necessarily intent upon existing things; yet the intellectual transcript of their condition, in that agony of attention, is only some intuited essence, some sensuous or logical term, which being their sole description for the object before them, they take to be that object itself in its whole existing nature. So individual forms of being stand in discourse for particular things. But sometimes, rather than some specific thing, a certain equilibrium of influences absorbs attention: a noon pause comes in our labour; and more special sensations being fused and blurred, we endure dull strain and duration without diversity —a vast, strange feeling. We return, then, as it were, to the sleep preceding life, to the peace of the womb: there is vitality without urgency, pressure without light, potential movement without object or express

*The sense of existence is not the intuition of pure Being.*

direction.  Such, we may fancy, might be the inner sense of matter: perhaps some forms of animal or vegetable life never yield any other experience.  A vague world is posited as existing; for in expectation and intent, as in memory and the sense of movement, there is a tacit assumption of things removed, threatening, eventual, as yet unknown.  There is accordingly nothing pure in this sense of existence, simple or vague as its deliverance may seem; for this vagueness and simplicity are uneasy.  The peace of the womb is precarious; it is but a muffled and initial phase of distraction, confusion, hope, and fear.  Care fills its heart, as it does our dreams; and we might identify it with the Universal Will of German transcendentalism, vaguely pregnant with worlds and worlds.  But slumber is not contemplation, and the buzz of matter Profound is not the beatific vision.  The pleasure, if contrast pleasure be found in it, is that of original sin: between the sense the father of lies is whispering in that paradise. of existence The intuition of pure Being looks in the op- and the intuition of posite direction.  In order to reach it, attention pure Being. would need to abandon all concern for transitions, events, ulterior or external facts, and to concentrate all its light on the positive intrinsic nature of the present datum; nor would that suffice, but from this special essence it would need to pass to the inner essence of all those alien half-known things, all those absent times, and eventual passions, which animal faith may posit, or fancy may conceive; since pure Being resides in them all equally, no less than in the here and now.  The force of insight would thus have to vanquish all will and transcend all animal limitations, cancelling every fear, preference, or private perspective which a station now and here would involve.  In other words, in order to reach the intuition of pure Being, it is requisite to rise altogether above the sense of existence.

The reason for this lies in the very nature of existence, which is flux and, as Plato would say, non-being.

Flux eludes intuition. The more truly existence is felt, therefore, the less possible it is to concentrate attention on anything, and to say, Existence is this. He is closest to existence, and most at its heart, who lives on the wing, intent always on the not-given; and even when the present fact is atrociously absorbing, as in pain, the sense of existence remains empty essentially and indescribable, by the very force and distraction of its presence. If we are asked to describe it, we are reduced to naming the circumstances or using some metaphor; and if in the midst of it we pause to consider the internal character of that which we feel, raising it thereby for the first time to distinct intuition, the distraction, the belief, the assurance of existence which filled us before have *ipso facto* disappeared: some image, some word, some finely shaded sensible essence alone is left. In other words, the proper nature of existence is distraction itself, transition at least virtual; so that it cannot be synthesised in intuition without being sublimated into a picture of itself, and washed clean of its contradiction and urgency. The relations which were external from the station of each of the parts as it arose separately, now become internal to the system of the whole; and the intuition in which this whole is synthesised drops the flux of existence in order to retain only its form and the truth about it.

If, then, being and existence seem in common parlance almost interchangeable terms, it is only so long as their respective objects are merely named The one is primitive, the other ultimate. or designated from the outside: when they are conceived positively and at close quarters they turn out to be exact opposites. Existence exists by virtue of oppositions in the place, time, and exclusive characters of particulars: being has being by virtue of its universal identity. This is true of the being of each individual essence; and it is true preeminently of pure Being. Its identity is omnipresent and internal everywhere; it equalises those centres of existence which in their single blindness become nests for external relations; it makes all times simultaneous; and by excluding change renders existence, from its point of view, inconceivable. Moreover, in reducing all things and all external relations to their internal being, that is, to their essences, it transports them into a realm of being which is necessarily infinite, in which their presence, therefore, is no temporary accident, as is their existence in the world: so that the existent becomes continuous with the non-existent, and neither more nor less real than any other eternal essence.

This contrast between being and existence is indicated by calling being pure. "Pure" is an epithet proper to all essences. Objects become pure when intuition permeates them and rests in them without the intervention of any ulterior intent or cross-lights, as we speak of pure mathematics or pure pleasure. Purity of this sort is no thinness of form, but the perfection of it. It admits any amount of detail, if it is all overt and clear, on the plane of actuality, and not latent. In this acceptation of the word "pure", pure Being is no purer than any other essence, but all are pure in so far as they are considered in their proper character, freed from the irrelevancies that may encumber them when they figure for a moment in some material world or in some labouring mind.

*Every essence is pure, by its freedom from adventitious relations.*

It would therefore be useless and redundant habitually to speak of "pure Being" if nothing were meant save that Being is an essence. What is indicated is that pure Being is related to other essences very much as any essence is related to its existing

E

manifestations; for whereas any special essence, such as colour or sound, sky-blue or B flat, is exclusive and definable by contrast, pure Being is present in them all, somewhat as space is in all geometrical figures, at once permeating and transcending each of them; for this essence, if not fertile casually as facts are fertile, is in its own way infinitely pregnant. The nature of pure Being anywhere implies the whole realm of essence, since being could not possess its full extension if any sort of being were forbidden to be.

Pure Being is so, by its freedom from internal diversity.

That pure Being, in the sphere of essence, should have this simple, intense, and pervasive sort of reality, provokes afresh in the minds of dialecticians that tendency to identify essence with existence which is native to the animal mind. For in the natural world too there seems to be an omnipresent, simple, intensely real something which dwells in particular things, is transmitted from one to another, and compels them to arise in their infinite variety and endless succession. This omnipresent something is called substance. Might not then pure Being, which lies in all essences and therefore also in all existing things, be the substance of these things, and the universal internal cause of their existence? This is a suggestion which has worked powerfully in the thoughts of those metaphysicians, like the Eleatics, whose physics has been dominated by dialectic. Nor is the suggestion altogether false. That something exists, that there is a world, is very true; also that whatever else this world may be, it is substantial—that is, exists in itself independently of all report or opinion. The hypostasis of being into substance is therefore no error, but a first awakening of curiosity and belief, which in so far as it posits the existence of something errs only by its extreme inadequacy. It honestly sets about using the category of substance, but without

Easy but fatal confusion of pure Being with substance.

any notion of what, in detail, this substance is. This
inadequacy itself is inevitable: how should animals in
the womb, or just out of it, conceive truly that constitution of the world which is not disentangled even to-day
by science or philosophy? Positive error only appears
when this natural inadequacy of our ideas is denied,
and when mere being is deputed to reveal the whole
substance and complete reality of things. The belief
in substance, which should have been the beginning of
art and science, then suddenly makes an end of them;
for if there were truly nothing in nature or in experience
except mere being, all events and appearances would
be sheer illusions, since in reality they would be all
identical.

I shall return to this subject in considering the
properties requisite in any substance fit to subtend
appearances and the life of nature; such Examples of
a substance must be unequally distributed Parmenides
and in motion; its proper name is matter. and Spinoza.
Here I will only notice in passing how the notion of
pure Being is likely to be contaminated in the effort
to identify it with substance. Pure Being—as is indicated by calling it infinite and eternal, if we ponder
these epithets—is utterly absolved from all sub-
servience to contingent facts and to the momentary
casual forms of human experience; it is the most
immaterial, untameable, inexhaustible of essences. Yet
Parmenides—no tyro in dialectic—denied that it was
infinite, because it had to give body to an existing
spherical cosmos; and indeed, apart from ancient
astronomy, existence always involves a certain concentration and contrast with what is not, and thereby
excludes infinity. Again, we find Spinoza asserting
that the entire nature of being—which he actually calls
substance—must be manifested in existence, and that
all these manifestations must be parallel to the forms
of the material world, of which indeed those other

manifestations can be only complementary aspects, by chance unknown to us. Here is the cosmic frog prodigiously swollen in rivalry with the ontological ox; but the ox, lest that ambition should seem too absurd, is accommodated to the frog nature, and pure Being is thought of as a sort of matter or force resident in natural things and lending them their existence, while at the same time enriching them with an infinite number of attributes which they hide from view.

On the one hand, then, if pure Being is substance, existence must be illusion; and on the other hand pure Being must be, not the infinite essence which it is, but a hard kernel for existence. Hence the sea-saw in the views of those meta-physicians who hypostatise pure Being; some-times their substance annuls all particulars, and sometimes it supports them. Pure Being excludes particular determinations within its own bosom, but it does not annul them in the world, because it is not on the plane of existence at all: it is by no means a matter within particulars which lends them existence. Substance, on the other hand, is such a matter; and by its movements and redistri-bution it gives rise in turn to every fact and relation in the natural world. Were pure Being an existing substance, nothing else could exist or arise, not even the occasional intuition of pure Being. All that exists exists by being other than pure Being, under circumstances which themselves are particular and contingent; and if substance were not contingent, un-equally distributed, and in motion, it would evidently not be the ground of any event or of any actual appearance.

*Substance is thereby deprived of its natural function, nature is abolished, and pure Being is obscured.*

Thus the hypostasis of pure Being, after being fatal to the reality of all facts, is fatal to respect for pure Being itself; because, considered as a substance, it would be useless, unknowable, and nowhere to be found. Pure Being, although a supreme degree of detachment and concentration be requisite to conceive it adequately, is, like any other essence, perfectly open to intuition; its sublimity is not obscurity; and it is excluded from "knowledge" only in the sense in which any immediate object, being an object of intuition, need not and should not be posited as a removed existence, by the transitive and precarious sort of knowledge by which facts may be known. But pure Being hypostatised into substance is a metaphysical spectre: matter congealed, arrested, emptied, and deprived of its cosmic fertility.

Pure Being, conceived as a substance or an existence, might indeed almost justify the well-known gibe that pure Being and pure nothing are identical. This sophism is complementary to those misunderstandings; the same misplaced preoccupation with physics has ended in impatience of logic and of honest intent. Of pure Being, which is not a romantic object, *Pure Being identified with nothing: psychological character of the latter idea.* the moderns have little experience: the idea of nothing is easier and far more familiar to them. We all know the feeling of contrast and disappointment which comes over the senses when they are robbed of their habitual entertainment, as, for instance, the sensation of darkness when the lights suddenly go out. The psyche, continuing to live her incessant life, feels cheated of her food and bereft of her employment. This is perhaps the origin of that horror of non-existence which afflicts so many mortals; a horror which would be evidently objectless and impossible if really nothing existed, and the poor wights were not there to shiver in the cold. But the psyche, feeling or imagining the sudden disappearance of her supports, finds her own existence empty and abortive: she does not know where to turn or what to expect, and this anguish is her acquaintance with nothingness.

For experience, then, "nothing" means a void caused by the absence of some expected thing.   The fact that such a thing fails to exist is logically dependent on the reality of its form of being, its designated and recognisable essence;   and the sense that there is nothing there, is dependent for its existence on a psyche missing some particular thing, and feeling a specific emptiness.   Negation, no less than doubt, assertion, or faith, requires the prior individuality of ideal terms;   and to predicate non-existence is in that measure to recognise essence.   Being and the non-existent here actually coincide;   not because both are nothing, but because both are being.   If all existence could be abolished, all essence would resume its equable reign:   and the absence of rude emphasis or blind exclusion would leave the infinite variety of being subsisting in peace:   although this fullness, even if an animal imagination could conceive it, might seem nothing to it, singly preoccupied as it must be with the flux of facts.

*Non-existence, partial or total, presupposes essence and leaves it standing.*

The fact of non-existence, then, is a natural alternative to that of existence, in many cases familiar, and in others feared or desired.   Like every fact, it is contingent, coming and going at will, and leaving the eternal manifold of being exactly as it was.   "The non-existent " is accordingly not a bad name for the realm of essence, seen from the point of view of existence.   But this point of view is adventitious;   no essence is non-existent intrinsically, since for all it contains or suggests it may very well exist;   that is, some existence somewhere may for a time embody or manifest it;   and even if this contingent occurrence were by chance perpetual—if, for instance, the essence of Euclidean space were frozen into an omnipresent everlasting fact in nature—this persistent accident would not touch the status of mathematical space in its

own realm, a status which is simply irrelevant to existence and not contrary to it.

When the word "nothing" denotes non-existence
it is fundamentally exclamatory: it expresses a feeling
or an encounter rather than an idea.  But Privation or
the same word may be applied descriptively not-being
within the realm of essence, to express non- presupposes
being or privation of essence; "nothing", defines it.
then, means "nothing of that sort".  This mixture of
privation distinguishes every essence, since in being
itself it is necessarily no other.  This is true even
of the most comprehensive essences.  A statue which
includes the head excludes the special individuality of
the same head reproduced in a bust: the different
limits individuate not only the two material blocks
but the two compositions.  So the realm of essence,
which is the full-length portrait of being, while it
contains everything, drops in everything that isolation
which makes it, when taken singly, seem the whole of
being: it shatters the illusion of so many philosophers
that they have found "the only possible" this or "the
only possible" that.

Indeed, the essential mixture of privation in all being
is more uncompromisingly evident among essences than
among existences, because existence, in ad- Change and
mitting change, seems to have found a way of existence
circumventing definition.  The expedient is cannot elude
essential
not successful, save in so defining an existence limitation.
that it may include successive phases, as a man's life
does: but both the incidents and the life still depend
for their being on their essential exclusions.  The
bachelor becoming a Benedict does not succeed in
combining contraries; his singleness is gone; any
backward glances or truancies which he may indulge
in only spoil and deepen his married state, in which
he then feels henpecked or adulterous.  Wisdom lies
in voluntary finitude and a timely change of heart:

until maturity, multiplying the inclusions, up to the limit of natural faculty and moral harmony; afterwards, gladly relinquishing zone after zone of vegetation, and letting the snow-peak of integrity rise to what height it may. Becoming, therefore, does not unite being and privation more closely than being unites them in itself, even without change or existence. The full character of each essence is inevitably absent from every other essence; but this relative privation or absence of what is alien is the consequence of possessing a positive character. Had each term no private, indefinable, positive essence of its own, it could not justify those exclusions by which we define it, nor could it fill its appointed place and spread out its eternal intrinsic relations in the realm of essence.

Pure Being, like any other essence, is individual and distinguished by exclusions, for it excludes those limitations which render all other essences specific; somewhat as light, which fills up and dynamically constitutes all colours, nevertheless excludes each particular tint. This is far from being a reason for calling pure Being a non-entity: the exclusion of all exclusions renders it infinite, not vacant. Vacancy and nothingness are terms applicable to existence, to which external relations are indispensable, and which at any moment may lapse, so that the place thereof knows it no more; they are meaningless in respect to essences each of which, including pure Being, is grounded in itself, and like a jewel or a star, shines all the brighter in isolation. Non-entity figures, indeed, in the realm of essence, because it is eternally impossible that anything there should be anything else; there are therefore always many things which anything is not. This non-entity is purely relative; an absolute non-entity would be self-contradictory, a false suggestion of discourse like the round square or the son of the barren

*Privation is a relative non-entity, but absolute non-entity is an impossible term.*

woman.  You cannot make a void of the realm of
essence, as you so easily might of existence, by waving
a magic wand.   Its indestructibility is not an accident,
a stubborn matter of fact, like that of matter or of God.
If you flatter yourself to abolish the realm of essence,
you actually refer to it and reinstate it;  if you deny it,
you affirm it.  The only negation of it which, in one
sense, might be staunch, would be utter oblivion;  but
oblivion is subjective.  It destroys nothing save the
feeling or thought by which something was formerly
recognised.

All essences, therefore, partake of non-being, and
pure Being does so in an eminent degree, since it
excludes the special forms of being proper to Pure Being
all the others.  Bread partakes of non-being is infinitely
by not being meat;  but food, or pure suc- positive.
culence, partakes of it doubly, by not being either
bread or meat specifically;  yet it is the positive being
in both, in so far as they can sustain life.  This pure
essence of food is something positive, present in both
but limited to neither.  Pure Being, like all essences,
rejects alien attributes by virtue of its positive character.
When an infinite amount of entity has been denied of it,
an infinite amount remains, compelling those denials.
For the relative non-entity of all essences comes to
them in so far as they exclude one another's characters,
whereas the positive character of each is its share of
being; and pure Being, far from falling outside, is the
absolute being in each.  It is also the totality of all,
when they are regarded not in their distinction (in
which they form the realm of essence) but in their
continuity and in their common latency within the
essence of pure Being itself;  because we may say
(though such language is figurative and inadequate)
that pure Being contains all essences within itself
virtually or eminently, since, though it cannot be any
of them, it requires each of them to be what it is.  The

essence of food (for we are not talking of accidental facts) requires and includes all substances that could be turned into flesh and blood. The very non-exclusiveness or intensive infinity of pure Being opens the way for all essences equally, and, since each is something, cannot suffer any of them not to be. It denies each because it remembers all.

In some sense, evidently, pure Being is the supreme being: may it, then, be identified with God? I think *It is not an* that a religion is possible which should have *existence or* pure Being for its object, and that it might *a power;* even become a popular cult; Brahmanism, *therefore* *not the God* as the initiated explain it, seems actually to *of theism* be such a religion. In theory it is entirely *or of pan-* *theism.* directed to identification with Brahma, that is, to eluding all finitude and existence; and the Mohammedans have a somewhat similar discipline, in so far as they abstain from all petitions, and cultivate absolute conformity to the will of Allah. But human religion inevitably has another side. Prudence and piety require a wise man to study the ways of nature, to cleave to good and to eschew evil. Among Greeks and Romans, Jews and Christians, the object of worship is fundamentally a fostering power; God is a dominant force in nature, creating, thundering, issuing commandments sanctioned by rewards and punishments, and in his inner being conceived to be a spirit, thinking, willing, loving, offended, and propitiated. A piety of this sort tends towards natural religion; its superstitions, if it remains superstitious, are superstitions about fortune; forces and events are its sole objects of reverence, and pure Being is nothing to it. The very earnestness of the fact-seeker compels him to reduce all myths as far as possible to literal science. Salvation he will identify with prosperity, eternity with survival, God with nature, or with some flattering purpose seeming to preside over human destinies. Divine commandments, or the will of God, will become in his lips merely an archaic phrase for the discoverable conditions of human well-being; divine omniscience will become the truth of things, and divine love their friendliness and beauty.

This makes a perfect religion for the irreligious; it means death to the spirit; but the spirit is not so easily killed. Action, like physical life, is free to *Yet in* perfect itself, if it can, in its own plane, ad- *natural* justing itself absolutely to its conditions and *piety spirituality* carrying out all its impulses in harmony; this *intervenes.* executive success, far from abolishing consciousness, will clarify it and make it musical. As the flux of matter, however self-contained and self-forgetful, cannot avoid casting an eternal shadow of its every phase upon the page of truth, so physical life cannot, by becoming very economical, avoid kindling all the more brightly the light of spirit: natural existence has these spiritual extensions, whether it will or no. And in respect to the realization of pure Being, ultimate and supremely difficult as it is to achieve ascetically, instinctively it lies curiously near to the simple heart. Wherever there is peace—not the peace of death, but that which comes of liberation from constraint or distraction—there is a beginning of spirituality. Consciousness is nothing but intuition thwarted or achieved. Even distraction, until it disrupts consciousness, is tossed between intuitions; it can therefore turn into contemplation at any favourable moment, by the mere suspension of animal will, anxiety, and care. Certainly the dark peace of the womb is far removed from the peace of the mountain-top, all clear articulation and self-consuming vision; yet animal consciousness, when perfect, is not unspiritual. It may rest on nothing more recondite than a warm heart or a sound digestion, or the overwhelming magic of some absolute lure: yet in its contemplative simplicity, in its disregard of all ambushed alternatives and material threats, it brings a foretaste of superhuman sympathies, which discipline might one day render disillusioned and habitual. When the object is pure, the spirit intent upon it is pure also.

Hence that strange solace which so many millions find in their religious devotions; under some disguise of fable or image, pure Being is their sanctuary from the world and their liberation from themselves. Natural religion itself, when reflected upon, drives them in this direction. Force and fact are reverenced by the humanist because in them he finds the sources of his happiness; but as he watches and studies them his reverence changes its hue; it becomes disinterested, sacrificial, liberating. Contemplation, even of destiny, neutralises the will. The exuberance of nature, the disproportion between her wantonness and the clean interests of man, must give the humanist pause; he will find the world cruel, and he may react on its cruelty by asking himself what thoughtless pledge he has given to it, that he should be subject to these vain torments. His piety will still forbid him to rebel against fate; rebellion would be a fresh form of vanity. There is no reason why man, or the transitory world in which he finds himself living, should have any prerogative amongst the realms of being. Traditional religion, for all its motherly coddling of human conceit, is not without a door towards the infinite. Theology must somehow reconcile the special mercies and graces coming to men from God, with the immutability and eternity attributed to him. Nor is this an idle theoretical question; for of what ultimate use would the graces and mercies be, if they did not lead men to share that immutability and eternity? In order to keep well and live long hygiene is better than religion. If the fear of power—that is, of matter—was the beginning of wisdom for the natural man, the possession

*Contemplation of pure Being is the last phase of spiritual progress.*

of power cannot be the end of wisdom for the spirit; and the spirit will not permanently worship in God a life inferior to that which it enjoys in itself. Power is a relation between existences; but where did existence and power come from, and how long will they last? There can be no safety in existence even for the gods. Safety in a living world means only forgetfulness of danger, because perhaps, on the scale and in the habitat of that particular being, danger may not be imminent. True safety, spiritual peace, profound reconciliation with fate, lie in another dimension: they spring from a new and superhuman direction of the affections. Piecemeal, amid the accidents of existence, ultimate good is attained whenever the senses and the heart are suddenly flooded by the intuition of those essences to which they were secretly addressed: synthetically, for perfect recollection, it is realised by the contemplative intellect absorbed in pure Being.

This absorption, the union or ecstasy of which mystics speak, has always been the goal of religious discipline in India, and wherever else the spiritual life has been seriously cultivated. This union is sacrificial, like that of the insect in its bridal flight. In it the spirit loses its self-consciousness, the sense of its own or any other separable existence: and it loses this existence actually, because it cannot attain that ecstasy without dropping all connection with its body—that is, without dying. The body may subsist afterwards automatically, or perhaps generate new sensations and dreams; but these will not belong to the liberated spirit, which will have fled for good, fled out of existence altogether. It would seem, then, to unspiritual apprehension, that the end of spiritual life is an end indeed: it is annihilation. This is the plain truth of the matter, when spirit is regarded from the outside, psychologically and

*The perfect realisation of it is incompatible with continued existence.*

historically. Intuitions are placed and dated in the natural world by their occasions and their organs : an actual intuition of pure Being—something absolutely infinite—is evidently irrelevant to any place or time, and disproportionate to any natural organ. We may safely say, therefore, that it cannot exist. Yet if we transfer our point of view to that of the spirit itself, and energise with it and by it, we shall see that intellectually and morally the spirit is fulfilled by the being of its object, not by its own existence. The soul, says Aristotle, is everything that it knows: but then, we may add with equal truth, the soul is no longer itself, nor a soul at all. There lies the selfless nature of intellect, that existence is indifferent and imperceptible to it, either in other things or in itself: so that in losing its existence—if it has died victorious—it has lost what was no part of its prize, and in attaining its prize it has saved itself entire. Certainly a song that ends full in the quieting of all its impulses and the synthesis of all its notes comes to an end just as truly as if it had broken down in the middle; both the soul saved and the soul lost cease living in time; yet what a strange blindness there would be in giving to both the same evil name, and making no difference between dying defeated and being perfected in death! If in the act of union with pure Being the spirit drops the separate existence which it had before, it drops only what it wished to drop; its separation consisted in not having yet attained perfect intuition, which must be without a natural centre or personal perspectives. On attaining that intuition the spirit abolishes itself by passing into that which it wished to find. Whether saved or lost, liberated or dissolved, the soul ceases to exist equally; but this fact does not touch the interests of the spirit seeking liberation, whose office, even from the beginning, was worship, not thrift or self-assertion.

It is only when we have thoroughly renounced self-

assertion and thrift that we can begin to understand
the spiritual view, which otherwise might seem to
contradict what the psychologist knows about spirit.
But there is no real contradiction: there is only a
transference of exclusive attention from one plane of
reality to another. Wherever spirit exists, it exists at
some particular place and time, by the operation of
its natural organs; but wherever it thinks, it regards
only some essence, eternal and non-existent, a more or
less ample manifestation of pure Being. It is perfectly
possible for any one who will consider the realms of
being together, to honour each in its place and to disregard the scorn which those who have eyes for one
only must needs pour upon the others.

If, then, contemplation of pure Being ever becomes
the last secret of a religious life, it does so only when
religion is transformed into a purely intellectual and sacrificial discipline. Positively
religious or moral feelings then drop into
their very small, very human places. Where
otherwise would be the transforming force,
the sublimity and sure finality, of this insight?
No fond eulogistic words such as "high",
"deep", "living", "spiritual", "true", patter any
longer about it; they have lost their afflatus and their
contraries have lost their sting. It is not because the
sage finds more in pure Being than pure Being itself
that he aspires to union with it, but exactly because he
does not find more. The fervent estimation in which
he held it before he possessed it would render possession
of it impossible if it continued afterwards. Like every
other object, pure Being appears under the form of the
good only to those who are moving towards it, or are
carried away from it against their will. Both creation
and contemplation are vital processes which lend a
relative value to their chosen ends; and when in a
religious life the end happens to be union with

It implies
no precepts
or scale of
values, and
does not
command
the worship
which it
may receive.

pure Being, this union becomes as precious and as legitimate as any other natural end could be to any spirit, but in no way more legitimate or more precious. Pure Being itself is neither ruffled nor flattered by these opposite currents in the flux of existence. Its authority—if we figuratively assign authority to it—cannot be invoked by either party, but both parties, like everything actual or conceivable, have its connivance and silent toleration. The artist and the moralist may shudder at pure and infinite Being, and may diversify and limit it in their own spheres to their heart's content; but understanding also has licence to be; it, too, is free to choose a good and perhaps to realise it; and it may weave again all those diversities and contrasts into the seamless but many-coloured garment which wraps Brahma in his slumber. There no praise or dispraise can intrude; all this flutter of spirits escapes from it unheeded and returns to it uncalled.

Here, before leaving this subject, I beg the reader to allow me a personal confession, lest he should misunderstand the temper in which I approach these speculations. Every pursuit has a certain warmth about it and sees its object in a golden light which, from that point of view, is a part of the thing discerned; and he who so sees it can hardly avoid using disparaging terms in regard to those who miss that revelation or are indifferent to it. So any artist in regard to his art, or any patriot in regard to his country. For the same reason the intellectual or spiritual life, especially when cultivated in unison with some long-established religious tradition, sets up its precise standards and prizes them absolutely: whatsoever satisfies other ambitious seems to it either a stepping-stone in its own path or else sheer vanity and illusion. Nevertheless it would be senseless to demand insight

The estimation in which pure Being is held is optional and relative to some finite nature.

of a stone; in the spiritual life there is nothing obliga-
tory. Those who have spirit in them will live in the
spirit, or will suffer horribly in the flesh; but this very
insight into pure Being and into the realm of essence
shows that both are absolutely infinite, the one implicitly, the other explicitly; they therefore release the
mind from any exclusive allegiance to this or that good.
It is only by the most groundless and unstable of
accidents that any such good has been set up, or any
such world as that to which this good is relevant; and
only to the merest blindness does *this* world or *this*
good seem absolute or exclusive. Now it would be
stupid in a blind man, because he was blind, to deny
the greatness of a painter who was admittedly supreme
in his art, or the sanctity of a saint, or the insight of
some thoroughly trained, purged, and disinterested
intellect; yet that blind man would by no means be
bound in his own person to begin for that reason to
paint, to pray, or to go into the Indian wilderness and
contemplate pure Being. Humility in these respects
is not incompatible with freedom. Let those excel
who can in their rare vocations and leave me in peace
to cultivate my own garden. Much as I may admire
and in a measure emulate spiritual minds, I am aware
of following them *non passibus aequis*; and I think their
ambition, though in some sense the most sublime open
to man, is a very special one, beyond the powers and
contrary to the virtues possible to most men. As for
me, I frankly cleave to the Greeks and not to the
Indians, and I aspire to be a rational animal rather than
a pure spirit. Preferences are matters of morals, and
morals are a part of politics. It is for the statesman
or the humanist to compare the functions of various
classes in the state and the importance or timeliness of
various arts. He must honour the poets as poets and
the saints as saints, but on occasion he is not forbidden
to banish them.

F

# CHAPTER V

## COMPLEX ESSENCES

By one of the uses or abuses of the word *is*, one thing
is often said to be another. This absurdity (as a
Essences pure logician might think it) flows out of the
are self- natural relation of essences with things and
defining. serves clumsily to express it. A thing
naturally has many appearances—lights, sounds, tem-
peratures, perspectives; and it may conventionally have
many names. Each of these essences, as it crosses
the field of intuition, is verbally identified with that
thing; but good sense, unless a sophistical attempt
at accuracy trips up its honest intentions, will easily
perceive that none of these names or appearances *is*
the existing thing; nor are they the existing thing
when added together, but still only a collection, indefinitely variable and extensible, of its names and
appearances. The thing is a strand in the flux of
matter which, apart from all appearances and names,
passes at its own rate through a continuous series of
states, until that strand merges into others and the
substance of it goes to form other things. So a man,
or other natural being, has a material continuity, from
birth to death, apart from the sensations which he may
desultorily cause in others, or in himself, and apart
from the names which he may receive.

Loose logic, incident to such naming and recognition of things, runs over into human thinking even

about essences, because these first attract attention as
signs for things, or as sensuous names; and it takes
time and speculative faculty to discern their intrinsic
nature.  If five potatoes go to the pound, those five
potatoes are said to *be* one pound of potatoes ; and it is
quite true that "five" and "one" are in this case alternate descriptions, in different conventional terms, for
the same parcel of matter.  Yet conceived apart from
that material signification, "one" is evidently not "five",
nor is number weight ; and when essences are envisaged directly, in abstraction (as people say) from all
that is irrelevant to them, nobody would be tempted
to identify one essence with another, or any essence
with any changeable thing.  Why confuse obvious
objects by trying to interpret or transform them at all,
as if their entire and individual nature were not given
in each instance from the beginning?  If the obvious
defies description, it does not require it.  Only it
happens that language, and the other laborious instruments of life, being addressed to the medley of things,
distract us from the obvious and render it ambiguous.
We form the habit of asking what a thing is, a habit
absurd if extended to essences.  Essences do not need
description, since they are descriptions already.

Nevertheless the attempt to describe certain essences
instead of simply inspecting them has some justification and meets with some success.  There
are memorable ideas which we may wish to      Essences
revive;  incidental means of reviving them    not given
may be at hand, since intuition has a         in intuition
physical basis determining the essence that   may be
shall appear.  So written music is a means    reported
of reviving melodies;  the phonograph is      circum-
another;                                       stantially.
and even verbal descriptions and similes may not
be useless in suggesting musical essences and distinguishing them clearly in their own category.
Intuition is thought, and anything that clarifies

thought enriches intuition. Less artificially, by the innate phonography of the psyche, much that is not given at the moment may be adumbrated and felt to lie in a certain direction within predeterminate limits of character. The intuitions with which the psyche is pregnant would actually arise if the living process that would generate them could be carried a little further: so our convictions are big with eloquence and our passions with predestined objects, which even if never realised are a sure unconscious criterion for accepting or rejecting anything that may be proffered in their name. The most interesting essences, like the thoughts of ancient philosophers, may be at some remove; how should they be known in their absence except by description? The imaginative inquirer is reduced to retailing the circumstances or to specifying sundry qualities in which the intended object presumably differs from those within his ken, until he catches or thinks he catches a glimpse of the essence sought.

An ulterior essence may thus be approached as a thing is approached, by laying siege to it and attempting to conquer it bit by bit; and the same

Knowledge of removed essences is problematical like knowledge of facts.

uncertainty always hangs about the most confident success in such an endeavour; because although the mind possesses at the end the essence it possesses, it cannot know that this essence is the one intended, possessed elsewhere by an intuition numerically different and historically remote. The entire historical study of ideas, of which romantic idealism is so fond, is irrelevant to ideas. Interesting as may be an improvised reconstruction of things past, and fascinating the learned illusion of living again the life of the dead, it distracts the mind from mastering whatever the past may have mastered; it inhibits pure intelligence, and substitutes for it the pleasures of sympathetic fiction.

Those ultimate visions are missed on which pure thought would rest, and which lend its only interest to rambling experience ; and even experience itself is surveyed in a false perspective, created by the special frame which the present provides for it, a present always casual and new; so that ancient history needs to be rewritten from the beginning by each generation of romanticists. Indeed, the object of interest in such reconstructions is not a moral revelation, not the re-discovery of an essence formerly discerned or prized, but only the fact that people once entertained some such idea ; and naturally the dates and the names of dead men become more important, and are easier to determine, than the truths or beauties which they may have known. Essences here, as in physics, serve only to supply names for divisions in the flux of matter; for after all this flux could not be distinguished into phases at all unless some essences were discerned in it. It is for this reason that minds fundamentally without loyal-ties, and incapable or fearful of knowing themselves, pursue subjects like the history of art or of culture. The illusion that they are interested in things beautiful or noble accompanies their purely material investigations, and they trace the genesis of every school of life without understanding the life of any, like eunuchs studying the physiology of love.

The first precaution, therefore, which the descrip-tion of a removed essence imposes is to discount the method of approach, the position and habit of the observer. He must beware of repeating here the error common and excusable in the perception of things, that of hypostatising symbols and hastily identifying views with the objects viewed. He must not project, for instance, on a complex essence like Euclidean space, the emo-tional simplicity of a blue sky or a dark room, nor upon a simple essence like pure Being the miscellany of those

*A complex essence may be indicated simply, and vice versa.*

natural facts or human ideas by which pure Being may
be manifested to him.  The most complex approach
will not complicate that which itself is simple, the
setting will not carve the jewel; nor will the blank
wonder of an eye seeing only simple bulks remove
complexity from the intrinsically complex.

In what sense can any essence be intrinsically complex, seeing that every essence has its eternal and
Three kinds indivisible unity?  This question will answer
of unity: itself if we ask another, namely, What is
qualitative, unity? because if there is a unity incompatible
quantitative,
and formal. with complexity, there is another essential to
it.  Pure unity is qualitative, like that of a scent or a
note, or like that of pure Being.  Such unity is indivisible and defies analysis.  But a pure quality may
pervade a continuum: the scent may be diffused, the
note prolonged, and pure Being may be contemplated.
The unity of this continuum is quantitative and
merely specious or imputed; it subsists because by
chance the component parts of it are not discriminated.
A continuum offers an opportunity for variation and
the interweaving of qualities — something impossible
without a common medium or field; quantity will then
become order, it will display a form or system.  The
imputed or specious unity of the continuum will not
be in the least jeopardised by this internal complexity;
on the contrary, the complexity presupposes the unity,
otherwise the elements would not figure in the same
context or fall into those relations which knead them
together into a particular compound.  These elements
would then remain separate simples, like colours in
tubes; before they can form any picture a canvas or an
eye must compose them into a complex essence, itself,
like every essence, perfectly single and individual.
Thus a third sort of unity, that of order, system, or
form, is presupposed in any actual complexity of
being; and the doubt whether an indivisible and

eternal essence can be complex dissolves in the fuller insight into what essence means. This complexity is not material; it is not the factual coexistence of elements themselves self-centred and self-existent. It is the essential complexity of a form, in which the relations of the parts are internal relations in the whole; so that both the total unity and the contrasting parts are pure essences. *A particular complexity is of the essence of most essences.* Every landscape seen, as actually seen (not as confusedly supposed to exist semi-materially like a natural stage-setting) is an eternal and indivisible unit; the least derogation from its complete essence substitutes a different essence for it. *That* spread of light, *that* precise emphasis of line, *that* mixture of suggestions, are no material facts collected into an existing object; they form the very individuality of the composition momentarily intuited, which any one who would ever behold the same landscape ("the same", spiritually speaking) must evoke anew in its perfect identity.

In most essences complexity is obvious: a line is drawn-out-ness, progression leaving a trail; a direction is a goal of progression chosen among others avoided. Every articulated image offers some spatial or temporal pattern which is essential *Complexity may be infinite.* to that essence. There is no limit to this complexity in unity: the system of any world is one essence; the whole realm of essence is one essence. There is therefore one essence which is absolutely infinite in complexity; but doubtless many others are infinitely complex in particular respects or categories, as number is; they would seem no less hostile and exorbitant to human imagination.

The reader must forgive me if I repeat a warning; a certain lofty and idealistic sound in the word essence should not tempt his tender mind to *Inhumanity of essence.* regard essence as somehow more human than matter.

Let him be disabused; the friendliness of essence is not intrinsic to that eternal sort of being, but hangs on two circumstances : one, that being non-existent, all essence is *innocent* and incapable of injuring or threatening him materially; the other, that when actually given in intuition, every essence is *luminous* and not estranged from him by any doubt or veil. Matter is neither luminous nor innocent; it is therefore no object for contemplation; but nevertheless there lie all his hopes; hence he sprang, on that he feeds, and there he must leave his mark if he would render existence more friendly to the spirit. It is by the shifts of matter, in the world or in the brain, that essences are revealed; very few can appear to human intuition at all, and still fewer to a sane human mind; happy the man who, in bringing to light those which to him can be enlightening and congenial, leaves all the others to loom for ever in the distance, like ancient gods respected but not worshipped: monstrous, tedious, occult, and inhumanly complicated.

In essences actually given the complexity possible is limited by the intellectual scope of the thinker; and
**Poverty of human intuition.** this is not great. Man, harassed as he is by pricks of fortune and irrelevant calls, has to rely on the organisation of his thoughts to make up for their poverty; if he does not misread his signals he seems intelligent, though his spirit may be a blank or stream of ticking trivialities, like the sound of the telegraph. The greatest men hardly have one great moment; their minds seem great only when the historian reviews their various actions or accomplishments, and pieces together a mythical source for them which he calls a great mind. There was never an actual greatness, a living thought mastering and directing the whole; and the historian himself is as incapable as his hero of gathering up that desultory competence into an actual intuition of the whole achievement.

Eloquence, or the spell of some rite, serves at best to hint at such an unrealised greatness; and man must commit to monuments, to books, to institutions, the suggestion of those visions which he never had. So seeds carry over from generation to generation a labouring something which we call life; it has an inward determinate potentiality, there is something which it would be; but when and where, in what joyful bridal or victorious cry, is that potentiality realised? The best seems still more than half hope and a strange uncertainty; and when we look at our clearest thought, at our most comprehensive intuition, we find in it almost nothing: we are always at cross-roads in a narrow valley, the whole world but a vague object of faith, only this poor halting-place actually ours.

So much is nature the mother of spirit, a child at the breast; it must be fed at every turn by things, resigning to their ministry that authority which it can-  Spirit is not exercise over itself.  These things, when great only great originally or made great by material by virtue of labour, first suggest to the spirit what ought its objects. to be its stature, if it aspires to comprehend them.  It is they that keep it plodding in the path of progress, and compel its lantern - light to creep wonderingly over their vast breadth.  Thinking is like telling one's beads ; the poor repeated mutterings of the mind compose, beyond themselves, a single litany, a path leading humbly step by step, past every mystery, up the mountain of knowledge.  It makes no difference to posterity how violent or prolonged may have been those effervescing thoughts which left this sediment of habits and institutions; what still matters is the seed-like power in this sediment, when stirred afresh, to generate in other spirits intuitions purer, juster, more classical than those into which nature might have budded untaught.  The syntheses of art are far greater and more comprehensive than those of life. If many poets had collaborated to produce the works of Homer or of Shakespeare, these works would still be what they are: in any case, each poet is many poets in act, as many as he has moments of poetic inspiration; and the psychic continuity of his animal person, crammed full of idiocies and vain prose, is far less rigidly pertinent to his message than is the material collection of his works. Material works, customs, and ceremonies are the stay of the mind; in them it grows sober, madcap that it is in its dreams; without them its fine thoughts would go out like sparks, accruing to nothing and transmissible to nobody. Even such familiar unities as we all profess to survey clearly—a landscape, a political event, a system of philosophy—are commonly unrealised mythical objects: we observe some casual feature and implicitly assume a system of other features which we might observe *seriatim*, had we the time and the patience; and the prophetic heat with which we hail this reality is out of all proportion to our actual understanding. We are satisfied if we can go on believing that the hidden truth would justify our sentiments, could we survey it synthetically; and what we call our knowledge is really only a string of miserable phrases and small points, supported by the rash conviction that behind them lies a great truth, a familiar friendly reality from which we are never far and about which we are never wrong.

There has been much play of dialectic (for instance, in the *Parmenides* of Plato) about the One and the Many, without ostensible result. Unity and plurality are essences; they find an obvious and, up to a certain point, a sure application in things: to which circumstance they doubtless owe the clearness and confidence with which we conceive them. But they cannot be expected to be the intrinsic essences of anything existent; the ex-

The One or the Many, if hypostatised, make an impossible physics.

istent will be many and one in a thousand ways without being one or many absolutely. Pure unity cannot exist, because existence by definition involves external relations, which will render many variable assertions true of that unit; and it would be by virtue of these relations, not of its inner unity, that such a unit would exist. If the One exists, then, as Plato says, it is Many. But if the Many exist, they are also One, since they could not exist without mutual relations which would bind them into one system. There are other reasons or relations which justify the same dialectical paradoxes: for instance, in so far as the Many are many, they are *each* one, as well as being One in their totality. There is no natural end to this shuffling of aspects; in the realm of existence, as Heraclitus and Hegel have urged, unity is manifold. Things are without other individuality than that which they acquire by proxy when some essence is embodied in them; and as substance is indefinitely plastic and forms are infinitely various, this world is much more emphatically a medley than a unit; and yet it is one in some respects, as in its dynamic continuity and in its speculative totality or system. An extreme violence is done to nature when such simple ethereal essences as unity and multiplicity are hypostatised. The result is a metaphysics which excludes the possibility of any physics—that is, of the only element in metaphysics which describes matters of fact; and the more intense the realisation of these essences is in intuition, the farther the contemplative mind flies from nature, and from any understanding of existence or any belief in it.

When, however, an essence with some precise articulation actually appears in thought, the alleged conflict between unity and plurality is perfectly solved, or rather is proved never to have existed. Suppose that in an architectural mood I stop really to consider and

*In given essences, they are correlatives.*

survey a façade ; could it, in an æsthetic sense, be a
façade if it was not one composition? Could it be
a composition if it had no parts? Could it be this
individual composition if not composed of precisely
these elements in precisely these relations? Of course
I am not speaking of the stones and mortar and
their chemical constituents ; from them, as from the
instruments of an orchestra, are wafted to me certain
material influences which kindle my intuition and, at
this juncture, evoke this vision. I am speaking of this
revelation of a moment, of something homeless in the
world though visiting me there under the gracious
influence of this place and hour; I am speaking of an
essence. I am satisfied if in respect to any and every
essence all cavil ceases, and it is heartily acknowledged
to be just as much one and just as complicated as
it happens to be, the complexity being complex
because synthesised in a single medium, and the unity
specific because composed of just these elements,
merged or contrasting in just this manner.

This perfect and eternal individuality of every complex essence is a point worth meditating upon; it helps
to make evident the infinity and, so to speak, the
democracy intrinsic to the realm of essence, and the
admirable absence from it of such things as scale, transition, genesis, or contiguity between its members. I
say, between its members, because of course *within* one
essence or another these relations, like all other forms of
being, are bound to be contained. Duration, specious
time, change, repetition, etc., are all essences perfectly
open to inspection, if not to description; the idiosyncrasy of each is absolute; and when they appear, the
peculiar relation between their parts (which is their
very essence) appears within them. But this very
idiosyncrasy renders it impossible that one should
become the other, or be composed otherwise than as,
in act, it already is; in such suppositions we are shifting

our attention from the complex essence to be inspected and substituting some view of our previous experience or of the material conditions which we presume have brought that essence to our notice. These historical vistas may be true ; but they could not be so if the synthesis which composes the vista did not faithfully render, here and now, the method by which events have unrolled themselves then and there. The question of the truth or descriptive propriety of an essence is therefore a second question, entirely subsequent to the question, or fact, of what this essence is. That change occurs continually in nature is true; but only because in the essence of change we have given together, in a single image, the successive phases of an event which, when change is enacted, are necessarily alternative. This power of projecting given essences and assigning them to things as their characters or as their relations, enables discourse to thread the labyrinth of nature dialectically. Far from removing from the complex essences so projected and used their perfect individuality, it presupposes this individuality, to which it assimilates the untraceable flux of material events. Whatever, then, may be the history of nature, or the genesis of intuition in us, all the forms which nature may assume are ontologically equally primary, and all the essences that may appear in intuition are equally fresh and original.

# CHAPTER VI

## IMPLICATION

SINCE any essence is an eternal form of being, each is grounded in itself without reference to any other. All essences Thus the realm of essence is an infinite are indi- plenum or continuum, in which every essence vidual and self- is surrounded by others differing infini- sufficient. tesimally from it in character. This realm is an absolute democracy by virtue of the indefeasible right of every member to its self-made place in it; and whereas in earthly democracies it suffices to be born in order to acquire every civic right, in this celestial republic even those who have not taken that risk and trouble possess full citizenship. Nor is any one threatened here by the pressure of the hard-hearted majority, or by any rude government. Here is perfect anarchy in perfect peace. The population is infinite, no legislation is possible, and everybody is safe.

In one sense, indeed, the being of any essence implies that of every other; for if any one essence is assured of its being because it is a distinguishable something, obviously every other distinguishable something is assured of its being on the same ground; so that an infinite multitude of essences is implied, if you will, in the being of any essence. Certainly no essence can create any other or remove it or pre-empt its place, that ontological place being all that an essence is. To play the dog in the manger is proper to things; essences are always in their respective kennels. The principle of identity (when the accident of existence is disregarded) renders the number of individuals spontaneously infinite; but this principle is no force exercised somehow extraneously on individuals, or which they could pass on to one another. Nor will so liberal an implication ever help thought to pass from a given essence to any other essence in particular. The intuition of the essence to be thought of next, even in the most obvious inference or deduction, must be generated by the movement of living discourse, and by the circumstances of some animal life. Essences are unsubstantial: the psyche, or matter elsewhere, is the substance at work. The essence last thought of was an essence only; it can trail no consequences and involve no sequel. To attribute consequences to essences is superstition.

Such developments, then, as take place in nature or in discourse are all generated materially. As they were first initiated contingently, because some parcel of matter happened to exist at some place and time, so the phases they traverse afterwards are generated, if not by chance, by some impulse which happens to be native to that structure or to the material circumstances that feed and transform it. At every stage such a development picks up one essence and drops another; each essence, like Michaelangelo's statues lying unhewn in the block, is intrinsically no better fitted for existence than any other, and cries for it no more loudly. The choice, as in the case of the statue, must be made by the genial fertility of things already existing—the artist, his habits, his surroundings. The artist is alive; his surroundings are full of fashions and movements; all these existing motions have directions; they leap and mingle and disappear like rills down a mountain-side. The forms they create, they create spontaneously. The aspect they assume may be unprecedented; and even if

*Their emergence contingent.*

familiar, it is but a haunting essence, without power to
reproduce itself or to exclude any particular sequel.

Hence the earnestness and honesty with which the
defenders of free-will assert at once two incompatible
A side-light things: indetermination and power. They
on free-will. are expressing the life of matter, which is
indeed not determined exactly to reproduce its previous forms, but tumbles forward to fresh collocations;
and the power in it is truly internal—not a compelling
magic exercised by any fixed form, energising either
out of the past or out of the future, but indeed a potentiality or propensity within the substance concerned, a
part of that blind impulse and need to shift which is
native to existence; and as this universal dance was
groundless in the beginning, so it remains groundless
at every stage and in every factor, whether the figures
of it be novel or habitual. This groundless pervasive
power, with its tireless inner monotony and its occasional outward novelties, is matter thumping in the
hearts of the free-willists much more loudly than in
those of their opponents. Believers in necessity have
caught sight of some essence—a law or habit or rule
of some kind—which they make haste to clap upon
nature, as if nature had no further depth, and they had
touched bottom with their proverbs; as knowing people
are always incredulous of things not within their experience or their books. At some depth, and in terms
not at all on the human scale, nature may very well be
mechanical—I shall return to this question in its place;
but each factor in that mechanism would remain perfectly spontaneous; for it is not the essence illustrated
here that can produce the essence illustrated there.
One configuration cannot even suggest another, save
to an idle mind playing with the rhymes of appearance;
but substance throughout continues groundlessly to
shift its groundless arrangement. One inert essence
after another is thereby embodied in things—essences

inwardly irrelevant, and associated even in thought
only when thought has been tamed and canalised by
custom.  The method of this transformation may contain repetitions, and to that extent it will be mechanical;
but it will never become anything but a perpetual
genesis of the unwarrantable out of the contingent,
mediated by a material continuity impartial towards
those complications.  So the common man feels that
he is the source of his actions and words, though they
spring up in him unbidden; and he weaves a sophisti-
cated moral personage, all excuses, fictions, and verbal
motives, to cover the unknown currents of his material
life.  Philosophers are not wanting to do the same for
mankind at large, or even for the universe.

Any essence is a model of explicitness; it is all
surface without substance.  When it appears, it appears
entire.  How, then, should any essence have
implications?  Implication is something in
which obscurity and fate seem to be lurking;
if so, it must be something imposed on
essences by human discourse, leaning, not on logic, but
on the accidents of existence.  And yet in dialectic we
are supposed to be elucidating the meaning of pure
ideas without any reference to their truth, as if the
realm of essence were a second cosmos, or rather a
first cosmos, the eternal intellect or Logos of God,
pre-existing by a fatality deeper than any creation, and
imposing itself on every possible world.

By insisting on the infinity of essence I have, in one
sense, already discarded any metaphysical rationalism
which should attribute this sort of prior existence and authority to any system of logic
or grammar.  Essences are prior to existence,
but being infinitely various they cannot deter-
mine existence to take one form rather than
another.  Moreover, if there be a divine
Logos composed of particular essences or ideas forming

*No pure essence can have im- plications.*

*The realm of essence is no par- ticular Logos, logic, or grammar.*

G

a closed system, it is evident that other systems, differently compacted or anarchical, would appear in the background, since the Logos would explicitly exclude them from its own panorama: the pre-eminence of this Logos would therefore not be essential, but due to a quasi-existence, to a fact or an accident. This is perhaps the reason why Plotinus and the Christian theologians have posited the One or the Father to be the source of the Divine Intellect; as this Intellect is presumed to be specific, and not the infinite realm of essence, it expresses, by that limitation, a factual principle, a primary accident, existence, or power. Much in the same way the transcendental logic of the Germans, supposed to control existence, has to be referred mythically to a Will or a Deed itself an absolute accident. In contrast to such a Logos, the realm of essence forms rather a chaos than a cosmos. Any special system has alternatives, and must tremble for its frontiers; whereas the realm of essence, in its perfect catholicity, is placid and safe and the same whatever may happen in earth or heaven.

No essence, accordingly, can imply any other in the sense of excluding from the realm of essence the

*Implication and impossibility hang on an accepted order in nature.* opposite of the essence implied, or any different complement. From itself an essence may exclude anything; in fact, it excludes everything not itself; but when a thing or a thought is said to preclude another, this happens only by virtue of adventitious laws of nature. A man cannot be in two places at once, not because the two places are not equally habitable or perhaps present to his spirit, but because they are assumed to lie apart farther than the span of his body. In what passes for logical exclusion or implication such a reference to existence is sometimes covert, but often it is quite direct and undisguised. All hangs on the usual connotations of language, on presumptions about the course of nature, and on the *argumentum ad hominum* addressed to the mental habits of mankind.

Implication in the first instance is indeed a physical relation, like that of surface to volume; such a bottle implies such a quantity of wine. Implication is the tacit commitment by which all the material detail and destiny of an object becomes relevant to intent when we point to that object or name it. So when a witness is called

*Implication may denote: (1) physical inclusion.*

up in court all his past, which may presently be unearthed in cross-examination, is implied and is set vibrating, as it were, by that summons; and this even if most of those details are then absent from his thoughts or perhaps unknown to him; he may be astonished to find, by the implications of the evidence, that like Oedipus he is a parricide. At bottom the same concretions in existence govern the deductions of logic. If in looking at an object I notice that it has three corners, this specious essence, three - corneredness, which is called up in intuition, becomes itself as it were a summons to all the other essences which might be found in the same object upon further scrutiny. I note next, perhaps, that there are also three sides, of a length not irrelevant to the breadth of the opposite angles; and all my supervening geometry will be developed, not by deductions from the original specious triangle, but by continued inspection and comparison of the forms of things. I may afterwards arrange my observations dialectically, re-defining my terms so as to include in them the material implications discovered in nature, as Spinoza arranged his psychology; the whole system will tend to become a single essence, in which all the parts are contained by definition; but my guide to the choice and discrimination of that particular system will be, and will remain, observation of nature. The truth of each term, and that of their arrangement, will be still empirical.   This is necessarily the case in regard to the *truth* of dialectic, at any level and in any degree of internal elaboration; because truth is subsequent to existence, being truth about it. Euclid or Plotinus or Hegel might be dialectical jewels without a flaw, and yet the whole truth of their systems would lie in the existence of a world which happened to exhibit the very special form of those systems with a miraculous fidelity.

Truth, however, is one thing and implication another.   May not one part somehow involve another

(2) Descriptive equivalence.
in a purely ideal system?   Yes; because, apart from material truth, an essence fixed in discourse at one moment may become an object of inquiry and intent at another moment. When these moments are continuous, or deputed to be continuous, the specious essence first given may remain sensibly the same, and yet may be re-surveyed and described in a new order, enriched by fresh analogies, measurements, or internal discriminations; and since all this subsequent analysis is but more inspection of the original essence, the new essences coming to light in the analysis (for they *are* new) are said to be implied in the essence analysed.   This is not strictly the case; the intuition of three-corneredness is innocent of the Pythagorean proposition and might be prolonged for all time without revealing it. But when geometry, the measurement of fields or of building-plots, has reached such a proposition, the mind does not lose its old object in the new, but superposes this upon that, and feels their identity for intent; the second is but an elaboration of the first, describes without falsifying it, and transforms it only by seeing it better.   In other words, a substitution occurs which is felt to be materially valid, especially when it may be reversed, and the two essences may alternate without inconvenience in the description of the same facts;

as sense and calculation continually relieve each other
in the practical arts. This reversible equivalence in
terms is something steadying to the mind; it is attentive science; altogether different from the stray
fertility of some fact or of some fancy, materially
dissipated in unreturning ways. In natural evolution
the original is destroyed, or if reproduced, as by a seed,
it is reproduced in a new instance, in a new setting,
with a destiny and a face never identical; but in dialectic the original theme subsists entire; it remains the
perpetual point of reference and criterion in implication;
its children surround it only to honour it. The most
mathematical triangle still has three corners; and all
the descriptions and analyses by which an essence may
be elaborated dialectically leave it as limpid as the sky
after navigators have crossed it with their parallels and
meridians, or painters have mixed their viscous pig-
ments to match its lights.

Implication, then, cannot enter into the realm of
essence or become truly native to an idea unless it is
turned into explicitness; that is, unless it (3) Logical
means the actual inclusion of a part in a whole. inclusion
The triangle, in so far as its three lines are of these
parts in this
included in the intuition which defines it, whole.
involves the lines so enumerated and synthesised; and
each of these lines, as found in that concretion and as
parts of that essence, implies the rest, as every stroke
in a picture, if taken as part of that picture, implies the
remainder. In other words, pure logical implication
is but analysis reversed, and subsists only so long as the
whole subsists and supplies the lines of tension and the
specific termini of those implications. But the moment
the given concretion is dispersed, the elements which
were parts of it stand alone, and no one of them implies
that whole any longer, or implies any of the other parts.
Neither the three angles separately, nor one or the other
of the sides, implies any triangle; each element is now

a complete essence, open to separate intuition, and not manifesting any need or proclivity to be united with any other essences into a whole centred elsewhere. Nor does it ask to be elaborated inwardly into any one of those patterns which might be introduced into it without destroying its outline and its present definition. Any such elaboration, if by chance it grows manifest, sets a new total essence before intuition, and abolishes the former object in its specious simplicity; for the outline preserved in the more complex essence, being but an outline there, is not the same actual object as the similar outline given pure and apart, though discourse may substitute the one for the other at its own convenience. Thus logical implication is unilateral; every essence involves its parts, considered as the elements which integrate it; but these elements, considered as separate essences and individual units (which all essences are) do not in turn imply any whole into which they may enter elsewhere; for they may enter into all sorts of concretions, and their only essential being is their own and what is intrinsic to their individuality.

Logical implication interests the contemplative mind because it enriches intuition; but the only implications that concern discourse are transitive

Nature gives play to logic in so far as continuity, repetitions, or fulfilments are to be found in her.

and therefore borrowed from the flux of nature. Wherever there is growth towards maturity or through some biological cycle, an eye familiar with that round may see in the earlier phases a promise of the later. The grub, for the naturalist, prophesies the butterfly, although presumably the essence of the butterfly is totally absent from the aspect of the grub and from its mind. There is only, I suppose, a mechanism which eventually brings about that complete transformation; but without needing to trace this substantial continuity, the naturalist may observe

the gross phases and outer habits of nature, as if forms
bred one another directly; and this regularity in
phenomena may become for him a sort of implication,
as the flight of birds became an omen to the attentive
augurs. In an empirical system causation is reduced
to superstition, skipping from fact to observed fact
without attempting to penetrate any of them or to
examine the medium which connects them substantially.
It attributes to a juxtaposition of appearances a
mysterious power to reproduce itself. Unfortunately
in immediate experience there are, strictly speaking, no
repetitions. The word *and* occurs often; but never,
for actual feeling, in exactly the same context, or with
exactly the same emphasis and colour. Empirical
philosophy, if sincere, ought to become mystical and
to deny that the flux of events has any articulation or
method in it. The fertility of being would then be
devoid of all implication; no involution would justify
evolution or give it direction.

Even a pictorial physics, however, may discover in
the flux of things something besides continuity: there
is inheritance. A son may not only appear as if by
chance in his father's family, but he may have his
father's nose. So in any moral heritage there is a
survival of early features in the midst of accretion
and change. The Old Testament is not merely bound
among us in the same volume with the New, but the
New quotes the Old, and the Old is said to prophesy
the New. In asking any question we demand a
relevant answer: the missing feature must not only
come into a given field but must somehow fit into it
essentially. A satisfying answer, while certainly not
implied in the question, responds to the essence of that
question in a way predetermined within logical limits;
it is pertinent. Pertinence is a loose or partial implication, as inheritance is a loose and partial repetition;
when these are added to continuity we have perhaps as

much logical coherence before us as can be demanded
of phenomena.

I have said that logical implication is explicit
inclusion of a part in a whole; but what is inclusion?
The
essential
elements of
an essence
are insepar-
able from it. When one essence is said to include another,
an identification has taken place *in discourse*
between an element in the inclusive essence
and the whole of the included one; but no
essence can *be* another, so that in this identification (which is the first principle and condition of
reasoning) there is something non-logical, not to say
absurd.[1]  We may say, and must say, if we discourse on
the subject at all, that pure Being includes unity and
that unity includes pure Being; yet if pure Being were a
part of unity, unity would not be one; and if unity were
a part of pure Being, pure Being would not be pure.
It is language and thought that create this confusion
by giving the same names, "being" or "unity", to
essences not in themselves identical; because the
being included in unity is not the individual essence of
pure Being: the nature of essence is pluralistic and
excludes pantheism.  So the unity included in pure
Being is not the individual essence of unity, but an
inseparable pervasive and unique something found in
pure Being by human intuition and identified abusively,
but inevitably, with the essence of unity when inspected
apart.  Identification is approximate only, and therefore inclusion is fictitious.  Not that identification
need be erroneous, as if, for instance, the unity in pure
Being were not truly unity but plurality.  Unity is the
right name for it; the essence of unity as contemplated
separately is the right one to assimilate to pure Being,
since in discourse assimilations are inevitable; but the
point is that the most proper identification is still the
act of calling one essences which are individually two:
a trick of discourse and language.

[1] Compare *Scepticism and Animal Faith*, pp. 111-115.

Thus pure Being is truly included in light, as in all essences, and may be discerned by intense attention in the given essence of light; but light is nevertheless not compounded of pure Being, present also to mere wakefulness in the dark, and a second factor, light without being. The second factor, whatever else it was, would include pure Being as much as the supposed compound includes it. Predication is therefore not a discovery of composition. As a thing is not a compound of its appearances, so an essence is not a compound of the terms into which it may be analysed. Analysis yields something specifically different from the object that justifies the analysis: an essence never *is* any description of it. Essences have no origin, and in that sense no constituents; their elements are only their *essential* features, which define them and are defined by them. A straight line may be intuited alone, say by an organic motor impulse felt in a dream: you traverse it, you have an immediate acquaintance with its absolute nature. You may think that you find it again by inspecting the edges of a triangle; but here the object, "straight line", has become the object of a different sense, sight, and appears in a context, the visible triangle, absent before, and strictly excluded by the original intuition expressing only a motor impulse within the organism. The identification of the straight line there with the straight lines here is therefore intentional only, not actual. It expresses an affinity between the two intuitions, their partial equivalence in discourse; and perhaps the separate occurrence of the first may have contributed, through the preparation and enrichment of the psyche, to the present complexity of the second.

Such conventional dialectic, in which intuition is submerged in the rush of animal discourse, is facilitated

Abstraction, analysis, and predication substitute fresh complete essences for the elements present in the essence considered.

by words and other rude symbols. Human intelligence is strangely materialistic, not in respect of matter, where materialism would be in place, but in logic;

*Logic is a path traced by habitual discourse in a field of relevant essences.* it begs of signs, which it assumes to remain materially identical, to assure it of the identity of the essences signified. Whenever we use the same word we suppose ourselves to have the same idea; and in any long or accurate argument direct intuition must give place to guidance by a conventional notation: discourse becomes a sort of calculating machine, by which material counters are shuffled materially and intuition is only required, if at all, to read off the result attained mechanically. Demonstration at best is something verbal and technical; logic is a kind of rhetoric. It marshals intuitions in ways which are irrelevant to them: in time, in the order of complexity, by analysis, or by synthesis; so it considers terms only from the outside, as if in the end everything did not hang on what they are intrinsically. Colour, for instance, being revealed by the same sense that simultaneously reveals extension, is felt to be inseparable from it, or even from the material object believed to exist in three dimensions. Yet colour in itself is a most pungent and positive essence, which can come and go while extension remains the same; and it is only an accident of human sensibility that no organ yields something which might be called colour without extension, as the ear yields high notes comparable to violet and low notes comparable to deep red. If this analogy were felt a little more strongly, every one might indulge in the licence of symbolistic poets who tell us that treble *is* azure and bass *is* crimson: they are only letting the cat out of the bag and betraying the secret that all identifications are matters of discursive impulse, intentional and poetical. Nothing *is* anything else; all essences, however complex, are individuals, and they are individuals, however simple. Their parts are parts only of that whole, as the right half of a picture is to the right and is a half only when the whole is given with it; otherwise it makes a whole picture by itself, and its centre is in the middle of it, not at the left-hand edge. But the simplicity of intuition makes the knowing mind impatient: it must get on, even if it gets into trouble. It loves generalities; but generality is a property *No essence* only of animal attitudes, or of names in *is general:* respect to the range of their application. *generality is* *a function* Many persons may be called John; many *of terms in* essences may be called triangles, including *external* the various definitions of the triangle itself; *relations,* for this is not a generality but an individual *dynamic* essence which is, or might be, discovered *physical* separately. It is not likely that the same essence *context.* should ever appear twice in human experience: of course, any essence *may* reappear, since it is a universal; but the complexity and fluidity of life make exact repetitions unlikely in actual intuition. The essences about which discourse hovers and to which it repeatedly refers are objects of intent, just as things are; they are common goals for miscellaneous vital approaches; and if an intuition of them were ever attained, intent and animal faith would still be requisite in order to identify the object present at the end with the object intended at the beginning.

The realm of essence, then, while it is infinite, continuous, and compact, nevertheless leaves *The* each of its elements entirely alone and self- *absence of* centred; it is the home of indelible multi- *all material* plicity and eternal individuality. No essence, *leaves every* not even pure Being, has any moral preroga- *essence* tive or any cosmic influence by virtue of its *innocent,* essential being: those functions belong to *inviolate,* contingent existences, by virtue of their *found.* dynamic relations with one another, which traverse and underlie the varying forms which they wear. Poetry and music lie as deep in the realm of essence as any logic; the thread of humour runs through it as essentially as that of fate. Pure sense has no object but essence; every contravention of human logic or natural law, as by chance established, is as firmly rooted in that laughing firmament as are Euclid and the Ten Commandments. A mock solemnity has too long made humanity pose as absolute; its virtues would be safer and more amiable if they recognised their relativity, and the spirit would be freer to recognise its superhuman affinities—because there is no reason why spirit should be merely human in its interests. Even nature likes to slip the gossamer bonds of human propriety and expectation, which entangle the fancy only of special individuals or nations; for matter resembles a lady often divorced, though never without a husband. The realm of essence is the playground of an even greater freedom, in a far more real singleness and integrity of being: because it justifies and exemplifies constancy no less than variety. Variability is hardly freedom, since it undermines the soul which aspired to be free. The desire to break away from an established system of life is after all a sign of weakness: the man has failed to become willingly and perfectly what he was attempting to become blindly. The truly radical liberty which the realm of essence opens before us is liberty to be something positive: as positive, precise, elaborate, and organic as it is in us to make it. Essence is an eternal invitation to take form. And the virtue of this invitation is not exhausted by being once accepted. All the possibilities remain always open ideally; and when the earth of a particular world quakes under it, and it fears to be lost for ever, its own essence, among the essences of all the other worlds, stands by in an ironical eternity, waiting for it to dissolve, and perhaps to be born again.

## NOTE

In this discussion I have endeavoured to keep my eye on the living subject-matter, and to make my language as plastic as possible in the description of it. But there are learned men whose notion of clearness is always to use words as they have been used before; they may find my view confused, and may ask indignantly whether I am a realist, a conceptualist, or a nominalist. Let me observe in the first place that even among the Scholastics these positions were held exclusively only by partisans and heretics; the orthodox doctrine included and required the three views in their respective places. Universals lay in the mind of God before the creation, and guided it. They therefore were *ante rem*. But according to classical natural history and morals, all created beings were inwardly addressed to determinate types, so that perfection and depravity were possible, and souls could be saved or lost. Universals lay therefore *in re*, and were the souls of things. Finally, human observation might gradually discover and define these universals, by giving a common name to their various instances as they appeared, for example, in disease or in beauty. Universals, for human experience, were therefore *post rem*.

Remove, now, the Platonic Ideas in their moral exclusiveness, and substitute an infinite realm of essence. All universals will still be prior to existence; all possible natural types, classes, or ideals will be found among them, as well as repeated in the pattern of nature; and every concept of thought, as well as every image in sense, will be found there also, and will be a universal. Universals are individual, not general: terms can be general only in use, never intrinsically; but the individual is an essence, not an existing particular. The latter is not a possible object of intuition and has no place in logic: it is some fragment of the flux of nature, posited in action, and by virtue of that status for ever external to thought. My position, then, is simply the orthodox Scholastic one in respect to pure logic, but freed from Platonic cosmology and from any tendency to psychologism.

# CHAPTER VII

## THE BASIS OF DIALECTIC

IF essences have no external relations, and therefore no implications, what can be the source of dialectic? When a man is inconsistent, we seem to distinguish that which should follow logically in his thought or action from that which ensues actually. Whence this distinction? And whence that systematic extension of concepts, so vast in scope and so specific, which the mathematician pursues, and which leads him sometimes to revolutionary discoveries? Whence that pregnancy in ideas, political or theological, which often renders them ominous, secretly absurd, and as it were hypocritical, having at heart implications which on the surface they disown?

The force and direction of inference cannot be native to essence.

The very notion of pregnancy gives, I think, a hint of the answer. Pregnancy belongs to matter, not to essence. The difference between what follows logically and what follows actually cannot be due to the conflict of two different orders of existence, one logical and the other natural. An existing logical order would be something metaphysical, a monster half essence and half force. The difference must be due rather to two levels of natural organisation, one cosmic and inanimate, the other animate and proper to the innate involution of the psyche in man, which opens to his imagination and reason paths other than those actually

94

traced by outer nature even in his own action or explicit discourse.

In the realm of essence, if ever we shake ourselves loose from our animal distractions and presumptions, everything that appears at all, appears patently; but in reasoning there is initially a hidden affinity or tendency in the terms, which does not become patent until the conclusion is reached. Then indeed the implication of those terms in this conclusion becomes clear, because they now simply define a new essence to which they are intrinsic. This new essence I know by intuition: no dialectic is involved in seeing or defining it to be thus. When the number *two* is given in intuition, the number *one*, repeated, is involved in it: this repetition of *one* is the very essence in view. But when the number *one* is given first, it is an accident whether I begin to count, and whether I go on living until I reach the notion of *two*. Therefore it is possible for me to define or deduce the number *one* by analysis when I have the number *two*, but not possible to define *two* when I have only *one*. On the other hand, it is quite possible, by living, to climb to the notion of *two* from that of *one*, but impossible to climb to *one* from *two*, because *one* is then already in my possession and under my foot.

I may observe in passing (confirming what I have said above about pure Being) that dialecticians who find in *one* the root of all numbers, or in the One the fountain of the universe, seem to be at heart less lovers of essence than of substance; they are not intent on form, but are searching for ultimate elements in the depths of time or of evolution, for something materially radical and indestructible in this existing world. High numbers do not satisfy them, and seem to them secondary, as they seem unreal or even humorous to idle human fancy: yet in the realm of essence all numbers are equally primitive and equally in the foreground. The parity and

The pre-eminence of the number *one* not essential.

eternity of all essences has hardly dawned on the minds of philosophers—at least not in the West.

Dialectic evidently involves transition; it is progressive; but any actual transition transcends the realm of essence (where every term traversed must always retain its intrinsic character) and proves that an existential and moving factor is at work, namely, attention and whatever may be the basis or organ of attention and of

Transition, repetition, and comparison are external to essences.

its movement. In a word, a psyche is involved, which herself involves (as we shall see) an existing material world. But dialectic contains more than transition, since this transition is often assumed to be a reversion; in reasoning, intent continually harks back to the object of a previous intuition and compares it with that of the present one. This feat is materially impossible; but it suffices if we perform it presumptively, by assuming that our successive objects are identical and that we should find them to be so if it were possible for us to observe them simultaneously. To transition, then, reasoning professes to add repetition and the assurance of repetition; so that besides a series of intuitions we must admit a power in thought which is not intuition but intent, since its object is something not given, but posited at a distance and identified in character only, not in position, with the given term. Intent is a sort of projection through faith, positing a relation of which only one term is given, the terminus or point of origin here, together with a gesture, word, or sense of direction indicating what and where the other term ought to be. This assumption—logically entirely in the air—is necessary to establish any instance of cogency, contradiction, or fallacy in reasoning; for the obvious disparity of two terms given simultaneously (whence comes all the emotional and essential assurance that the square is not round) does not prove any contradiction in discourse, until we assume that these very essences were present to some mind professing to identify them; and this assumption is very likely to be false, and is always hazardous. It is the great source of futility in argument. The first postulates of dialectic, therefore, the constant meaning of terms and the principle of contradiction, are rooted in animal faith. The light of intuition cannot avail to establish that use of them which alone renders them potent in discourse, or applicable to any subject of ulterior interest. The obvious is obvious, but terminates in itself; that which we say *must* be so, need not be so unless our habits of inference are independently justified by the course of nature.

Now that part of nature which is the organ of mind, the psyche, is a relatively closed system of movements, and hereditary; the living seed, as it matures, puts forth predeterminate organs and imposes specific actions and feelings on the young creature: he must eat, fall in love, build a nest, resent interference or injury. But this predetermination is not exact, only generic; the seed develops as it can, under fire of the environment; the psyche in each individual grows into a somewhat different system of organs and habits, and these vary with time, not merely according to the predetermined sequence of phases in the race, but according to the fortunes of the individual. This partial predetermination of life—which in man is especially imperfect, and dependent on the chances of education and experience—is the source of the generic; the general, absent from the realm of essence, is omnipresent in impulse and action. Every living creature aims at and needs something generic, not anything in particular: *some* food, *some* shelter, *some* mate, *some* offspring, *some* country, *some* religion. The impetuous soul, half-baked and addressed only to the generic, pounces on what it happens to find; it receives it into the stomach, or

Biological nature of the generic or general.

H

into the mind, and digests it if it can; but there remains
almost always a distinct disparity between hereditary
capacities and demands, in their potent vagueness, and
the satisfaction provided for them. *Not this, not all
this, not merely this*, says the psyche at every turn; and
her sustenance leaves her half-disgusted and half-
hungry. Experience at the same time clarifies the
instincts which it disappoints; and it is in terms of
actual perceptions, expurgated or transformed, that
secret ideals can first come to expression.

Dialectic is fledged in this nest, and obeys the same
conjoined forces of innate impulse and casual experience. Each thought, in its existence, is due
equally to the predisposition of the psyche
and to the course of nature outside; but
the *presumptions* inherent in the thought,
or accompanying and flowing out of it, are
determined by the psyche alone, by the
momentum and direction of her life at that moment.
Hence the whole moral conflict and tragedy between
reason and fact, desire and event, the ideal and the
actual, nature according to philosophers and nature
according to nature. In pure reasoning this conflict
takes the form of opposing relevance, consistency, and
implication to wandering thoughts or chance perceptions; but the force of logic, as we have amply seen,
does not reside in the essences actually inspected,
which have no transitive relations, but expresses the
habit and range of the psyche in the thinking animal.
A mind not buffeted by change, in a world in which
rain and shine were not alternate, would never think
of any complements to a present object; it might even
passionately deny their essential reality, and might call
China impossible, life in the water unthinkable, and
any morality but the familiar one self-destructive. In
minds, as in insects, the vehemence of littleness is re-
markable. Man although born plastic and immature,

The generic prejudices of the psyche are hardened and made specific by habit.

soon borrows fixed prejudices from casual experience;
he is teachable, and achieves littleness, or has it thrust
upon him by custom and dogma.  Acquaintance with
facts—and with how many facts is any man acquainted?
—narrows his generic native demands into specific
requirements; he must now have only *this* food, *this*
shelter, *this* mate, *these* children, *this* country, *this*
religion.  In the same way the mind, when indoctrinated, will suffer only *this* physics, and only *this* logic.
Nevertheless, any given world or any given flow of
imagination is an accident; its very character would
be inexpressible were it not surrounded in the realm
of essence with an infinitude of variations any one of
which, had it been realised instead, would have been
equally accidental.  Even the true sage, who passes
through the school of experience and learning only to
recover his spiritual freedom, cannot range impartially
over the realm of essence; the paths he traces in that
labyrinth are imposed on him by accident, because a
psyche is at work within him obeying special instincts
and biassed by a special experience.  Even in him the
transitions of dialectic and the course of contemplation
are not determined by the structure of the realm of
essence, since the realm of essence, by definition, is the
home of all possible structures.

Dialectic, then, while ostensibly following ideal
implications absolved from any allegiance to facts or
to actual instances of reasoning, secretly expresses a
material life, and this in two stages.  The psyche is
predetermined at birth to certain generic conceptions
and transitions; and these are rendered precise and
irrevocable by habits formed under the pressure of
circumstances.

Everything in dialectic hangs upon strength of soul;
it is an effort to carry over intuition from one moment
to another, to be true to oneself, and to wander
into no vision not congruous with one's first insight,

and complementary to it, so that at the end the mind may believe that it has gathered in and preserved all its riches, and unearthed the secret of all its objects. This is something which no living mind does or can do; and in so far as the ambition to do it is successful, the success is balanced by a great illusion, almost inevitable to the complete logician; the unity which his discourse has achieved he imposes on the realm of essence and on the existing world as if it drew their circumference and repeated their intrinsic order. This illusion does not destroy the dialectical coherence of the system which occasions it; but the philosopher probably aspires to describe the truth; and in that he fails, in proportion to the vehemence with which he posits his system, with its dialectical structure, in lieu of essence in its infinity and nature in her unknown depths. Dialectic is the conscience of discourse and has the same function as morality elsewhere, namely, to endow the soul with integrity and to perfect it into a monument to its own radical impulse. But as virtue is a wider thing than morality, because it includes natural gifts and genial sympathies, or even heroic sacrifices, so wisdom is a wider thing than logic. To coherence in thought it adds docility to facts, and humility even of intellect, so that the integrity of its system becomes a human virtue, like the perfect use of a single language, without being an insult to the nature of things or a learned madness.

*Moral function of dialectic.*

Being *a priori*, that is, being the assertion in the face of things of a pre-formation in the soul, dialectic is fundamentally romantic; but its romanticism may become austere and ascetic, in so far as it desists from professing to drag the world with it in its speculative flight. How far the *a priori* rules in a mind is a biological accident; we may imagine some insect or some

*A priori logic expresses physiological pre-formations.*

angel, created full-fledged, in whom it should rule exclusively; and we might perhaps find fanatics in whom it rules exclusively in speculative matters, once they have been thoroughly indoctrinated. For we must not suppose that anything is *a priori* in origin; every instinct and organ has its history, just as every custom has; but once the organ formed, it imposes *a priori* certain responses on the body and certain ideas on the mind. The *a priori* is such only in function. So when an intuition has become dominant, and has established its settled affinities in a well-organised mind, the further march of mundane experience becomes useless to the logician, or even distracting. As young poets on a slender experience sometimes reach the greatest heights and the greatest depths, finding nothing to intercept the impetuous flight of their spirits, so the dialectician who most resolutely hedges-in his thought in one lane of logic, may go farthest in that direction, and most unerringly. He unveils some integral pattern, perhaps never copied by things, in the realm of essence; the integrity of his pure intent and undivided attention have enabled him to unveil it. He has laid on himself the difficult task of being consistent, of being loyal, not to the realm of essence, which cannot be betrayed, but to his own commitments; he is determined to find and clarify the meaning of his spoken thoughts. Dangers lie to right and left of his path: he may slip into a change in his premises or into forgetfulness of his goal. Fulfilment is moral, even in logic. The mind bears burdens no less than the body, from which indeed the mind borrows them; and the pregnancy and implication of ideas are signs of that vital bias.

Intuitions are themselves incidental to animal life; in revealing the purest essence, like a colour or a number, they remain rooted in the soil, and render every image symbolic of the conditions under which

it arises.   Thus colour brings with it extension, form,
position, and an aerial emotional redolence drawn
from the vital influence of light and room

Intuitions
have a
natural
context
with which
the essences
revealed are
associated in
discourse.

upon the psyche; number suggests a certain
particularity in its units, as if it were a mere
aggregate, yet this particularity is proper only
to the moments or parts of existence and is
absent from the constituents of number in
its purity; for in a number the logical units
numbered are merely fractions of that number, not
particulars in themselves.   Yet these physical roots of
intuition are far from jeopardising the essential purity
of the flower to which they lend these human affinities.
Horticulture simply becomes more varied and expression richer.   Intuition lyrically marks the chief crises
in material life, when some organ composes and
accelerates its movement, turning it into a musical
note.   Dialectic is merely a change of scope in this
organic synthesis by which a new essence is substituted
for the one first given, that is, for the theme and terms
of the analysis or deduction; a change by which the
original essence, in disappearing, is identified with a
part of the new one, or with a whole of which the new
one is a part.   The transitions are discursive, their
necessity is merely psychical; but they lead to intuitions in which essences appear having intrinsically a
logical complexity corresponding more or less perfectly
to the stages of discourse which preceded; this corre-
spondence, so far as it goes, makes the validity of
dialectic, a validity which cannot be intrinsic to the
essence reached in the conclusion, since it is the
validity of a process, of a series of substitutions and
identifications.

Essences are related to dialectic somewhat as things
are related to experience.   A stock or stone, dead in
itself, may exercise a living influence on the imagination.   If I strike it, or if it falls upon me, or if I take

shelter beside it, I encounter a reality unfathomable in its complexity and pre-established in its station; but in my romantic experience it has become an enemy or a friend. So the terms of discourse, taken in themselves, are passive and complete, implying no development; but I have arrived at them by the quick exercise of my senses or by a concretion of elements in *The progression of discourse is a natural flux, controlled physically.* my thought; there is a history and a momentum in my apprehension of them, and it is by no means indifferent to me, as it is to them, how they shall be superseded or transformed. Most sequels open in the realm of essence (and these sequels are infinite), or even most sequels likely in a dream, would prove irrelevant to the interest dominating waking discourse, which is not these pure appearances but some problem in the material or moral world.

Discourse is not contemplation; dialectic is more laboriously intertwined with the accidents of existence than is intuition. It is selective, responsible, perilous; like everything in flux it moves forward by a kind of treachery to its parent world, and subtly pretends to fulfil that which it is destroying. The continuity is physical, not logical. The navigators who in the age of discovery followed in one another's traces or sought to outdo one another's exploits, had a common background and a common field; otherwise their new worlds, however marvellous, would have added nothing to the old world, and would not have discovered one another; America, China, and India would have retained their ancient self-sufficiency; while Castile and Aragon, England and Holland, would have grown no richer and no wiser. So with every problem, however ethereal. A problem is a natural predicament, a living perplexity, limiting the relevance of the solution sought and creating its value. Discourse would not be cumulative, it would set and solve no problems, if it did not share and express the adventures of a psyche in a material world; for the controlling force in reasoning is not reason, but instinct and circumstance, opening up some path for the mind, and pledging it to some limited issue.

Dialectic, like investigation, is a path to an end; it is instrumental. When successful and finished, it yields to intuition, for which the facts and relations discovered become an ordered system, a single complex essence. Then the predicament and the problem lose their malignity; they survive only in the interest or beauty which, in dying, they bequeath to the new object spread before the mind. Contemplation becomes disinterested, but remains pleasant; for it is not the contemplation of *any* essences at random, but of those precisely to which a vital affinity drew the current of my blood, the hidden essences to which my nature was directed, partly from birth, partly by ingrained habit and arts learned by experience. It is the consecutive sanity and moral integrity of a mind that hold it down to dialectical consistency. There are goals in animal thought, as in animal action and passion, of which thought, in its material basis, is indeed an integral part. These goals are set by the nature of the organs at work, a nature in its turn more or less adapted to its external opportunities; so that the goals of a healthy intellect—for instance, geographical knowledge—like those of hunger or love, are not unattainable, except by misadventure. When a geometer analyses the triangle or a lawyer points out the implications of an alleged fact, he is appealing to a fund of principles domesticated in the minds of his hearers, principles which he may call axioms or simply common sense. His dialectic will be cogent if it leads in the end to an intuition in which all the details gathered during the argument may find their places: that is, although the successive intuitions

*The end of discourse, intuition, is itself a function of animal life.*

and the essences they revealed will have disappeared, the stimulus and momentum which created them will proceed synthetically to a fresh intuition, as it were their joint heir, combining them without loss or friction.  This total intuition will perfect the operation of its organ, raising rational life at that point to its natural entelechy.  The many by-paths of fancy or logic either not traced or explicitly excluded will be called false or irrelevant; and so they will be in this final system to which they are logically repugnant; but they cannot be false or irrelevant in themselves, nor in such other systems as they might help to build up. These other systems are rejected, not by logic but by the structure of the psyche and of her environment. Thus Euclid clarifies the intuition of space which the Egyptian builders, and earlier perhaps their arboreal ancestors, had gathered in the prosperous course of their sports; Euclid brings to light the real implications of such building and such swinging.  His science guides those early arts to their ultimate self-knowledge. That those first terms of animal observation and this ultimate geometry are alike well chosen is a truth of physics and morals; their application is perfect in the fields from which they were drawn; they give the true rationale of human building and swinging.  But the realm of essence cannot suffer violence, and the constructions favoured by man or by nature do not prevent the same elements from entering, if occasion arises, into other designs.

The purely logical cogency of a system lies accordingly in the internal relations of that system when completed.  The included elements have no Absolute intrinsic obligation to belong to such a evidence system; but if they fall within the intuition is intuitive and internal of a living mind, which if well knit can have to essence. only one such ulterior system for its natural goal, they should be, and probably will be, addressed by that mind to that system.  Were the elements left detached, or combined into other wholes, the dialectic proper to that mind would be lost in the sands of a vain experience, and its congenial system would never take shape. If, for instance, any other man had undertaken to compose this book, it is certain that at every cross-road in the argument he would have taken a turn somewhat different from mine, without necessarily doing more violence to the elements combined.  Our systems might have been equally coherent, if in each case the elements became parts of a single essence, clearly intuited; but each system would have been a monument to a different spirit and a different life.

The value of two such logical systems for the description of nature would be a second and distinct question.  The more cogent system might easily be the more extravagant or childish one, if the elements combined were few or fantastic, or the harmony sought merely poetical.  On each animal species, on each man and nation, nature imposes a special way of thinking, and they would be foolish to quarrel with their endowment; they will not attain truth, or anything else, by eluding it. Their thought will issue in a coherent system if their original intuitions were sharp, the synthesis of them broad, and the interpretation honest.   Then all random trains of thought inconsistent with that system will be instinctively discarded; and through many a council and controversy, as in the formation of Christian dogma, heresies will be excluded as they suggest themselves, and the scattered original revelations will be interpreted in such a sense that the spirit which originally received them may honour them together.  Every science and language and religion is big with unsuspected harmonies; it is for the genuine poet or philosopher to feel and to express them.  Only an orthodoxy can possibly be right, as against the bevy of its heresies,

*Validity in a system can be only symbolic and moral.*

which represent wayward exclusions, or a fundamental disloyalty. But no orthodoxy is right as against another orthodoxy, if this expresses an equal sensitiveness to the facts within its purview and an equal intellectual power. All values are moral, and consistency is but a form of honour and courage. It marks singleness of purpose, and the pressure of the total reality upon an earnest mind, capable of recollection. The spirit of system, though it so often renders the mind fanatical and obdurately blind to some facts, is essentially an effort to give all facts their due, not to forget things once discovered and understood, and not to leave illusions and vices comfortably unchallenged. Certainly the total reality will elude any human system; but that is no reason why human nature, which is itself a system, should not exist and assert itself; and it cannot exist congenially without intellectual clearness or without translating its natural economy into a system of ideas. In the realm of essence no such system can have any pre-eminence over any other; each is the pattern of only one possible world; but it may be the full revelation which the existing world brings to one particular creature, and it may render valid, for his description of things, those dialectic bonds which are internal to it.

# CHAPTER VIII

### ESSENCES AS TERMS

NAMES are normally given to things rather than to essences, and are then proper names; that is, they are indications like a gesture, designating a natural object without describing it. Although words like " table " and " John " may be names common to many natural objects, each of these objects is an existence containing much more than the fact that it is a table or is called John; therefore in giving the name " table " or " John " to that object when encountered, I do not mean to distinguish an essence, either intuited or intended, but to indicate a thing distinguished by its position relatively to me in the natural world, and by its general potentialities and connections there. I do not profess, in so naming this object, to exhaust its nature, but merely to point to an existence in a certain quarter, with a casual, relative, and summary characterisation of it. I should indeed not call this object " table ", unless it were a piece of furniture of a certain height with a flat top; and I should not call the other object " John " unless it were a male inhabiting an English-speaking country; but these conditions for applying those names are far from being the objects; the objects named are particular, natural, fluid, and indefinable.

It is possible, however, to apply names to essences also, as, for instance, to the triangle or to beauty; and

*[margin note:* Words may be signs for things or for essences.*]*

then these names are inaptly called general. I say
inaptly, because they do not designate classes of things,
but in designating an essence they leave open the
question whether any or many things exist describable
by that term. Names then designate not particulars
but universals.

The application of names (or other signs) to essences
has an important consequence: it permits reasoning.
Things have no dialectical relations, their
very existence and fluidity being a defiance *Things,*
to dialectic. The unity of a thing is not *flux, elude*
perfect and definable, as if a thing were an *dialectic.*
essence hypostatised. It is a partial, dynamic, historical
unity, in that a thing remains traceable for a time in the
flux of the world; until according to the conventional
use of language that particular thing is said to perish.
Everything would be continually perishing, and nothing
would endure for two moments, if a thing were the
essence which for one moment it exemplifies; and
everything might be everlasting were a thing the substance which is transmitted, within the conventional
boundaries of that thing, from each of its moments to
the next. A thing is a part of nature, a mode of
substance, a parcel of matter that plays a certain part
and wears a certain mask in the comedy of change, and
only so long as it does so; when the same matter puts
on a new mask and begins to speak in another voice, it
has become another thing. Socrates is a part of the
flux of nature, between limits fixed by the birth and
death of one animal. Neither his aspect nor his
thoughts at any one moment are Socrates; and the
essence which his life embodies when taken as a whole
is also not Socrates, but is only the truth of his life,
seen under the form of eternity. His opinions may
have dialectical relations, but he and his actual faith in
them cannot have them. Existence itself is a surd,
external to the essence which it may illustrate and

irrelevant to it; for it drags that essence into some here
and now, or some then and there; and the things so
created, far from being identical with their essence
at any moment, exist by eluding it, encrusting it in
changing relations, and continually adopting a different
essence; so that nothing accurate can be said of a
thing supposed to bridge two moments of time. Yet to
bridge two moments, in some sense, is indispensable to
existence.

The essence of a process, if we turn to that, is also
not that process in act. The actual process is an
existence inwardly unstable, and all I have just said
of momentary being applies to any stretch of existence;
the span of any event is just as truly a moment as the
minimum duration which human wit can conceive.
Sense, history, science, and poetry are all in the same
case: they arrest essences, exclamatory visions, and
apply them as names to the flux of nature, which they
can neither fathom nor arrest.

Dialectic, then, though itself a movement in thought,
can weave together only eternal essences; and the
pattern it thus designs is an eternal essence
in its turn. In reasoning, attention passes
and re-passes between these fixed terms, and
if by chance any of the terms were exchanged
for another, the reasoning would be fallacious, becoming to that extent an irresponsible dream. Now
there is a psychological difficulty in reverting in intuition to exactly the same essence. In a mind so
volatile as the human, it is not to be expected that the
entire complex essence present at one moment should
ever be present again. The organ of thought being
in flux, the terms of thought can hardly be repeated.
The purposes of communication and reasoning would
therefore not have been served by attempting to name
and recall the entire actual burden of any moment.
Only in dramatic and lyric poetry do we approach any

Fancy, in
"breeding
flowers will
never breed
the same".

such effort at complete personal expression. Even here, of course, success in reviving or communicating a moment of actual life is never more than approximate. Readers of poetry feel that the poet has been well inspired, and that they have rekindled his very soul, if *any* full, new, and vivid moment of intuition is begotten by his words in their own bosoms; and the more the inspiration is the reader's, and not the poet's, the greater the poet is thought to be. The irony of fate in this may wound a man's vanity, who hopes to be immortal in his own person, and to impose his opinions or his loves on mankind for ever; but humility and elevation of mind (which go together) will not take offence. The poets have had their own visions, the truth and beauty of which are hidden in God; and their works have been so closely knit into the instruments and traditions of human expression as to be fertile there in many a new pleasure and fresh thought. Reasonable minds will not ask for more. Whether the exact intuitions which they have reached can ever come to any other mortal, is a question not even to be broached; for the function of poetry is not to convey information, not even to transmit the attitude of one mind to another, but rather to arouse in each a clearer and more poignant view of its own experience, longings, and destiny. To this end the elastic connotation of words, with the intrinsic dignity of phrases (as in the English Bible), is a positive advantage in poetry. It enables the same symbol to quicken images in various minds, according to their several capacities, stirring them to a true sincerity. Hence the musical, inspired, and untranslatable nature of poetry, which lies more in the assault, relief, and cadence of the utterance, carrying with it a certain sensuous thrill and moral perspective, than in the definable meaning of the poet's words.

In prose, on the contrary, words are primarily signs for some fact which they serve to record or announce.

The sounds themselves, and the other essences, emotional or pictorial, which in intuition convey such information, are passed over. They are mere

In specifying facts, intent is controlled by action.

instruments — the claw with which intent clutches the potent fact. Nor is the intrinsic essence of this fact that which, in prose, words profess to describe. It would be a vain speculation, akin to poetry, to consider what a stone, or a sheep, or an enemy may be in themselves: such a question would invite not to action but to self-forgetfulness and sympathy — a dissolving sympathy with dramatised things which is idle or even dangerous. I might soon find myself refusing to eat mutton, or going over to the enemy, or disproving the existence of stones. The tight mainspring of action and thought keeps me ticking without such scruples, or if they intervene, condemns them to futility. Prose, like perception, designates things only externally, things which, since they act and are acted upon, are substances. I have found that substances posited by animal faith are identified, not by specifying their essence, but by indicating their place and function in that field of receding events called nature, of which any act is the centre. The existence of nature is involved in the execution of any act, since this act is a link in a flux of events extending beyond it. At the same time belief in nature is involved in the intent and eagerness which in consciousness express action, or readiness for action.

Thus the profit of bestowing names on things and of speaking in prose, like the profit of being sensible at all to external objects, does not lie in revealing the essence of these objects, but in expediting action amongst them. The whole network of appearance and language may accordingly remain a miracle of æsthetic and grammatical design spun in its own colours and suspended in the air without inconvenience or anomaly, if the connections meantime established between action

and action are still quick and nicely adjusted.   The
whole rumble of the discoursing mind is music on
the march, and no sane man expects it to join in battle
or to describe the enemy fairly.

As music, however, may occasionally become an
object of thought in itself, and may be elaborately
described by the musician, so many an In specify-
essence which in the apprehension of things ing essences,
was only a symbol or an emotion may be controlled
arrested in reflection, and receive a name. by language.
The name, with its valence, so to speak, or its atmosphere of suggestion, now becomes the datum in actual
intuition;  and the essence which formerly occupied
that place and was a symbol for some material fact,
now recedes into an object of intent and a theme for
consecutive description.

Speech and writing are a complication in nature;
as they exist substantially they are subtle secondary
figures and rhythms impressed on matter, which serve
mankind to record or forecast those larger rhythms and
figures, called real things and true events, in which
human existence is itself implicated.   Thus language,
like sensation, becomes significant by virtue of the
animal faith which vivifies it; and this significance is
its moral being.   The same framework of spontaneous
belief, readiness, memory, and expectation on which
understanding of nature is stretched, stretches and
projects also the force of words, making them indicative
of absent and eventual objects.   If the object is an
essence, it nevertheless is identified only by being
placed in some natural perspective, borrowed by
language from the material world.   An absent essence
can be indicated only as the essence meant by a
sign, which is commonly a word, and the sense of
this word can be revived and realised only by reverting
in fancy to the natural environment in which it was
first uttered.

I

Thus description in words or other signs is indispensable for making an essence an object of intent when it is no longer, or not yet, an object of intuition. The torments suffered by the souls in Dante's *Inferno*, for instance, are not intuited by the poet or the reader in their intended essence, for then he would be enduring those torments actually: yet he knows what he means by them; the words or images that suggest them are significant, and in proportion as they are well chosen, they converge upon the object, the unrealised essence of those torments, as they would be if actually felt. Such convergence, while it might render the description perfect in the language used, would not at all tend to reproduce the pains, by bringing their essences into living intuition. On the contrary, it would be the essence of poetry that would actually fill the mind with verbal harmonies and sensuous vistas continually opening and closing; if there was any touch of repulsion or actual distress, it would be by a lapse from pure discourse, as when Dante becomes political, or a childish reader takes alarm, fearing that the material world may contain the bodies and places where such torments occur, and that there is danger of deserving them. In meaning an essence we accordingly by no means tend or wish to intuit it; but just as in the case of material objects of intent, we indicate its locus in the realm to which it intrinsically belongs, here the realm of essence as there the realm of matter, without at all requiring to create, in the realm of spirit, an intuition of that object as it is in itself.

It appears, then, that just as the whole world of common sense, history, and physics is posited, not experienced, so the whole world of dialectic—the labyrinth of essences studied in mathematics, logic, grammar, and morals—is meant and not intuited. Of course to posit any-

*Symbols have their own essences which alone are immediate in discourse.*

*Essences signified need not be intuited.*

thing is itself an experience, and in meaning something
I must have some intuition of my terms and some feeling of intent; but the actual experience of knowing is
not the object known, and the essence intuited in
reasoning about essences is not those essences; for
either the essence meant is a part only of the given
field of intuition, or it is not given at all, but indicated
by converging symbols as the object of an eventual,
perhaps unattainable, intuition. Thus $\pi$ is an essence
meant, which can enter unequivocally into an equation;
but it is not expressible in arithmetical figures, nor
in any sensuous experience; its nature is known by
circumstantial definition; it is a goal of thought, the
exact proportion between the circumference of a circle
and its diameter. When I think of $\pi$ this exact proportion is signified but not intuited: what is actually
before my mind is the Greek letter, its sound, and a
shooting vista into a world of words, human mathematics, breaking here and there into images of specious
circles, visual or given by gesture; a psychic sea
through which intent can nevertheless easily steer
towards the fixed but unattainable object defined as $\pi$.

Even when an essence is present, like the colour of
the sky, I must retreat a little and revert to it from a
different intuition in order to identify or to mean it; and
this different intuition is commonly that of the word
" blue ", the name of that colour. It need not be this
particular word: the Spanish word *azul* in my case
would do just as well; a fact which shows how separate
the intuition is in intending from the intuition in seeing,
and how disparate. Or possibly, in taking in or apper-
ceiving the evident blue and describing it, I may use as
a point of vantage the visual memory of some material
object, say the background of Titian's " Bacchus and
Ariadne", thinking to myself, This blue is that blue!
A wafted image, referred to some natural object, and
to the occasion and place where I encountered it (for

London and youth hang for me about that picture), may thus take the place of verbal predicates to define an intended essence and keep it as an object of perpetual reference. Merely to prolong a present intuition will never turn the essence presented into a goal of intent or a term useful in discourse; such a term must be kept constant in its absence, and must be often absent if it is to be always the same.

Intended essences thus acquire, through the machinery of identification, projection, and intent, a certain remoteness and mystery; they become concepts or ideals. Not that when they swim into intuition, if they ever do so, they are not perfectly individual and concrete;

*They lose nothing thereby in reality.*

this blue which now floods the sky and my own being is the most obvious of realities, and the nearest at hand. So, in its essence, is that blue which is now not here, but which I evoke sentimentally out of a remote context in the world of hearsay and of memory, and which I identify with this blue, because this blue has awakened in me a state of feeling and a train of associations, ending in a revival of the circumstances of that lost intuition and (as I fondly assume) in a recovery of that lost essence. *This* blue is still the only essence before me: that this blue was also *there* is an assertion not founded on a simultaneous inspection of the two objects, which is impossible, but on enveloping the given essence in the old atmosphere and calling it by an old name. This identification is hazarded: thought and belief (even if to be verified) are shots in the air when they are actual; but the irresponsible movement by which intent posits its object takes nothing away from the intrinsic reality of this object, be it a thing or an essence. I may, if I have the necessary indications, intend and refer to things in their absence, without compromising them or reducing them to abstractions from my present beggarly self.

Homer was better inspired in speaking of winged words than those philosophers who call words sounds or movements of the larynx.   Material organs and material occasions are no doubt indis- *The intrinsic flight of discourse.* pensable to the birth of language, to its evolution, and to its utility.   So a flying arrow requires a bow and a target, and the material reed and feathers that are its substance.   But discourse is flight, it is signification; and the more we scrutinise its actual being, the more unsubstantial, fugitive, and transitive its essence appears.   Not only can it never alight or become anything but a flying intent, but even the hits it makes (not to count the misses) are achievements only conventionally; it dies on arrival, and can never know whether it has killed its bird.   It is for the gamekeepers that follow in its wake to collect the bag; and how different is this dead booty of mundane routine and prosperity and plodding art from the gleaming flight, the intent aim, the miraculous shot of actual thinking!

If any one in his speculative ambition is bent on seizing the veritable essence of substance, I hardly know what comfort can await him; but if his satisfaction was rather in the patterns and harmonies of essence, which he hoped to disentangle dialectically, he need not be disappointed; because even if the terms of his demonstrative science are remote terms, always objects of intent and never of intuition, yet at this remove and in that shadowy precision they form an actual perspective, a present theme for the mind. Essences are omnipresent; and while attention remains awake, you cannot shut off one without presenting another.   If the objects of intent remain remote, as the persons of a novel and their career remain imaginary, the discourse which is the seat of those intentions must always be actual, like the crowding words, images, and excitements loved by the authors and readers of novels.   The medium is always immediate.

The life of language, of poetry, of dialectic, is a keen and an innocent life. It has, by virtue of its roots in

It circles with enough fidelity about the flux of nature. the body and the control of its development by circumstances, a quite sufficient relevance to material facts, a quite respectable value as a record and forecast of human destiny. Intrinsically it has its own vital, expressive, æsthetic intensities. It is not an illusion, unless it is turned into illusion by inexperience or equivocation. Love, for instance, arising irrepressibly in each successive generation, is a genuine revelation, not rebuked at all by the knowledge that it has often existed before towards other objects; if it involves illusions, they regard only ulterior facts, less important than itself. So the literary or mathematical or grammatical medium of discourse, with all the logical and moral zeal which it involves, is genuine life, full of intent and intuition. Why rebel against spirit, and ask it to be something other than it is? The flight of the arrow, in spite of Zeno, is as true a fact as the ulterior positions between which it flies or the rest which it dreams of but excludes by flying. So the intrinsic essence of discourse is signification, a flight in which the wings are words or other signs, alone actually present, and the goal, alone valued or considered, is descried simply as the point of the compass, perhaps receding and unattainable, towards which those wings are straining. It is in the act of traversing data in such a specific direction (to which a living animal holds much more unswervingly than to the intuition of any datum) that names, which are cries, come to the lips; and as these cries are habitual and very limited in number compared with the cloud-like drift of intuitions, they serve to mark the goals of thought far more clearly and unambiguously than its actual being. So things are better defined in discourse than sensations, and intended essences better than essences given.

# CHAPTER IX

## INSTANCES OF ESSENCES

SINCE pure Being is infinite and contains all essences, how can anything else be?  In other words, what is there in existing things besides their essences?

That this question can be asked is a proof that it is a legitimate question and admits of an answer;  for if there were nothing but essences, and if pure Being, because infinite, exhausted all possible modes of being, there would be no discourse, no ignorance, no knowledge, and consequently no questions.  In the realm of essence all equally is open, safe, and perspicuous: one essence cannot slily entrench itself on a sort of egotistical eminence, from which to survey, attack, or deny any other essence.   Since this, nevertheless, is done in what we call life or existence, and since I am doing it at this moment in this inquiry, it is certain that pure Being is not all being, and that in existence Being is impure, having in it something more or something less than any essence.  This is but another way of asserting that there is a world, that there are facts, and that there is a difference between truth and error.  Such a thickening and self-contradiction by which essences become things may irritate the dialectician and may disturb the contemplative mind; but any attempt to deny the fact would be idle; the denial itself would reintroduce the very

*Any instance of an essence proves that essence is not the only realm of being.*

categories of existence, flux, self-transcendence, and truth which it professed to dismiss. Could a man really be sublimated into his essence, he would be silent, as pure Being is silent. Let him who will by all means ascend into that blessedness, if he can; but he must leave philosophy to poor living mortals whose minds are crepuscular and in whose impure world much is past, much is distant, and all is obscure.

To pursue this subject would be to broach at once those realms of being which are not that of essence; *Exemplifica-* here I must leave the question of their *tion trans-* precise nature in suspense. But I can *plants* hardly avoid some examination of the effect *from their* which they have on the manifestation of *proper soil.* essence to the human mind; for in making this manifestation possible, they intervene in it, mingling with it an urgency and obscurity which no essence can have of itself. Manifestation is an event, and although that which is manifested there can be only an essence, the occasion and the setting transpose it into a new plane of being, the plane of phenomena or of descriptions, and render it, as the Platonists said, other than itself. It is intrinsically and inalienably eternal, yet here are temporal instances of it; it is a universal, but it appears in particulars, lending them such positive characters as they may have; it is perfectly unambiguous, and nevertheless it is merged and confused with other essences in the flux of things and of language.

Realisation of essence, by an ironical fate, is accordingly a sort of alienation from essence. We call it "realisation", when from being perfectly real in its own fashion, it becomes an illusion in some mind, or the momentary form of some treacherous matter. Or perhaps we call it "manifestation," when that which manifests it, some existing thing or phase of discourse, distracts us from it, and scarcely suffers us to observe it for its own sake.[1] Instances are indeed occasions for deviation: they are cross-roads at which two worlds meet. One set of relations exhibits the instance as an essence; another set exhibits it as a fact. The idiosyncrasy of the essence there realised alone enables the fact to be distinguished from the rest of the natural medium in which it exists; if we were interested in true being, in the actual and moral quality of things, it is accordingly that essence, and its essential relations, that would absorb all our attention. But we are animals swimming for dear life in the same flux in which this instance of essence has appeared: it is the movement of that medium, what will happen to us next, that preoccupies us; and therefore, probably, we neglect the intrinsic being of that occasion, and of all

[1] There are various phrases capable of expressing the relation between an essence and the instances of it; each phrase represents some perspective view of the same actual relation. We may call it *participation*, in that every instance shares with the other instances the whole nature of the essence; but this term may lead to misunderstandings, if we infer that an essence has parts, one of which may fall to each instance, or that an essence is a class or collection of particulars. If we express the matter in a religious myth, as the story of the fallen soul, instances may be said to *remind* us of a divine original, that essence in its purity; and then, in a cosmological myth, this original may be conceived as a magnet attracting matter (when matter is sensitive to that particular attraction) into a likeness of that essence; so that any existing instance of an essence might be called an *imitation* or *copy* of it. Such copies, if subsisting only in the mind, would be *recollections*. A less picturesque name for instances is *phenomena*, that is, *manifestations* of an essence; but these terms, for a modern, suggest a subjective seat for the instance, whereas of course many phenomena are manifestations of essences in matter: in other words, temporal things. A safer word for instances in general is accordingly *exemplification*. This covers both *embodiment* of essences in matter or in events, and *revelation* of essences in intuition. A synonym for exemplification might be *realisation*; but it has the disadvantage of suggesting that essences when not exemplified are not real, and that reality means existence; whereas unexemplified essences are perfectly real in their own sphere, and many of those exemplified, being only imagined, do not exist in the sense of being the forms of any substance. The term realisation is convenient to express the passage from an incipient to a clear thought, or from an unfulfilled to a fulfilled perfection in things; in the former case we may also say that the essence has been *defined*, and in the latter that it has been *materialised*. The great difference in all cases is that instances can occur only once, while essence may recur any number of times; that which is local in the occurrence is the instance, that which might be identical in various occurrences is the essence. If I write the same word twice, the word which is the same is the essence and the words which are two are its instances.

occasions, in our haste to trace one occasion out of another. The net of existence in which the instances of essence are caught even seems, perhaps, to our rude philosophy to create the fish which it catches: we deny their prior reality, their intrinsic being; they are to us only the contents of our net; and we shut our eyes as we swallow them. The matter of them may still nourish us; but our attention, to that extent, has deviated from the intuition of essence, which is its only spiritual function, into tracing the labyrinth of fact; we have chosen the endless path leading from existence to existence—as indeed any instance of essence, since it must come before us on some natural occasion, invites us to do. As in translating a language we must abandon it, so in recognising an essence we must half materialise it; in existence, in sense, and in thought it has become impure; its essential character now figures in a substance, a medium, or a context which are alien to it.

This incarnation of essences in particulars must not be supposed either to alter the essences (which are Instances all incorruptible) or to be an imperfect perfectly incarnation, so that a part of the divinity, so exemplify their actual to speak, descends into the world and another essences. part remains in heaven. Certainly in any assignable world or portion of a world only an individual essence can be realised; but of *that* essence the realisation there will be perfect. The infinity of pure Being renders it inevitable that whatsoever form an existence may happen to assume, that form will be some precise essence eternally self-defined; for however fast the world may change or however confused chaos may become, events can never overtake or cover the infinite advance which pure Being has had on existence from all eternity. And whichever of those prefigured forms a thing may choose to realise, that form it must realise perfectly; as an aerolith, if it falls to the earth at all, must strike some pre-existing spot on its surface.

So, too, in the history of existence, as it picks up and drops these multitudinous characters, there is also no ambiguity. Substance, in the act of taking on and shuffling these forms, merely connects them in a voluminous flux alien to their several qualities. The dance falls into figures and generates relations, which each essence taken individually did not contain or imply. *The birth of spirit complicates the exemplification of essences without confusing it.* And if further facts arise out of this movement, as spirit arises in animals, the characters and complexion of these hyperphysical existences are also just what they are; feelings and discourse take on such colour or intent as they have without dislocating in the least the order of nature which they enrich. The pearls may be inwardly more precious and opalescent than the thread on which they are strung; or they may seem superfluous and negligible to a science or action so economical as to trace the thread only; but whether prized or ignored, the pearls shine by their own light in their assigned places quite unequivocally. In a word, there is no ambiguity in the truth; it enshrines all the facts, no matter how complex, with their exact configuration. Inexactitude, approximation, imperfection, are not possible in the relations of things to their essences; each thing at each moment is just what it is; it is transformed as it is transformed, related as it is related; and the sum of these changes and of these infinite crosslights is just what it is under the eye of eternity.

Nevertheless, from the moral point of view, imperfect realisation is not a meaningless phrase. Imagination, language, and interest are finite; the categories of human discourse, though somewhat variable, are constitutional and limited; they need to be so in order to fulfil their cognitive and imaginative function, since knowledge is an adaptation of fancy to practice, a rational eloquence, not a reduplication of things as they were before life or imagination arose among them.

Confusion arises only when discourse assigns to things essences which are not theirs.

Every name and every desire accordingly suggests an essence to the psyche which may fail to be realised in the world, or may be realised there only approximately; the fact that another somewhat different essence is realised there leaves human attention cold; it asked for bread and receives a stone, and to point out that the stone was a perfect stone would seem sheer mockery. The disharmony between the psyche and the rest of nature runs even deeper; for the essence actually realised in the facts may be not merely unwelcome or uninteresting; it may be nameless altogether and inconceivable. Every name and every concept which bewildered man will impose on those facts will then fit them imperfectly; and being without intuition of their true essence, he will call them vague facts, formless, elusive, or defective. For his senses have their stock responses, like birds of one note, or of very few; so too the passions and the theories of which his imagination is capable. His discourse moves within a private museum of ideal and general natures, the few essences distinguished by language; and it is only in his finer or his idler moments (if he has them) that he looks between the meshes of that logical net, and catches unauthorised glimpses of the flux of things with all its irrelevant marvels. Essences, then, may be said to be manifested imperfectly, when they are not the essences of things, but are prescribed for them by the senses and passions of some egotistical animal whose mind is like a stomach limited in its powers of digestion and obliged to treat all foreign substances as approximations—how questionable and half-baked !—to its ideal victuals.

If, then, it is possible to assign to anything an essence which is not its essence, this possibility arises because

the essences first and normally manifested in feeling
and thought are not the essences that have been
embodied multitudinously and successively
in things since the beginning of the world,
and that now define their dynamic nature.
Yet merely this disparity between ideas and
things would be no anomaly, because
ideas are not things but ideas; and ideas,
like words, may be excellent signs for
events in the field of action, without in the least re-
sembling them, if only the mechanism which controls
these ideas does not precipitate any assertion, expectation, or attitude which events within or without the
psyche do not justify. The justification required is
not that the essence given in discourse should repeat
the essence embodied in material events—a repetition
which is unlikely, superfluous, and incongruous with
the summary function of sensation, as well as of significant or poetic thought; for in naming, reporting, or
prefiguring events, discourse will necessarily add an
intellectual syntax, a moral perspective, and a mocking
humour which are not in them. What is required is
such a vital harmony between the life of thought and
that of things as may render discourse appropriate
and adorning. But often — and here's the rub —
maladaptation exists in their respective movement and
rates of change between a psyche and her environment,
so that the essences revealed imaginatively to that
psyche are late or early or out of key with the march
of events, not only outside, but in the residual parts
of her own life. Then, in her assertiveness (since she
is engaged in action) she will impose on things that
which she adds, and deny that which she leaves out;
and this hypostasis of her fancies or of her ignorance
will become unfathomable error about the facts encountered by her in action and prompting her to this
fond discourse. Thus discourse, while manifesting

*Originality in ideas is a beauty but becomes a snare when they are used as predicates for things.*

perfectly at each moment certain specious essences to
the spirit, and embodying perfectly the essence of
spirit itself, may involve confusion regarding the objects
which it intends to describe, as well as ignorance of its
own basis, nature, and history.

In the study of nature philosophers are much in-
fluenced by the love of economy. They wish, on this
The error of subject, to have as few ideas as possible;
intellectual they may even hope to be monists and to
parsimony. have only one. This ideal of simplicity is
imposed on nature by the mind in its desire to be
clear, comprehensive, and curt; it is an extension of
the dogmatic impulse involved in action by which the
most conspicuous essence given in sense is taken for
the essence of the object encountered. The philosopher merely repeats this form of judgement when
he assumes that the simplest theory which his wit can
frame must be the essence of the universe. In the
study of essence, the ruling interest being more contemplative, we may perhaps avoid this haste. Illusions
are no less truly essences than truths are; and no confusion will arise from complications or diversities in
essences if only we abstain from asserting them of the
same substances. Now I believe that more essences,
and of more kinds, are exemplified in nature than the
student of nature is inclined to notice: they are not
realised only in single file or on one plane of being;
and they are not all predicable of the same substance
nor all predicable of anything. There are many open
to our inspection which are not descriptive of material
things even indirectly; and on the other hand, there
are presumably embodied in matter many essences,
of many kinds, which it has not entered into the heart
of man to conceive. Such considerations are not useless in stating, if not in solving, the problems of natural
philosophy; but for the moment I must be satisfied
with a word about the essences which must be exem-

plified, some in one way, others in another, in order that discourse may move at all, and ideas may describe, or fail to describe, their intended objects.

The character of the particular world in which we find ourselves has been richly and ignorantly reported in the poetry and science of all ages; it is *The essence* not for me, in passing, to revise those reports. *of this* There is avowedly a great inorganic cosmos, *world.* astronomical, geographical, chemical; and on earth at least there are living organisms capable of adjusting themselves progressively to their environment, and of modifying that environment for their future convenience. The essence of human life thus runs over and engages parts of the outer world in its rhythms, in what we call the arts; and this seems a miraculous subjugation of matter by mind. But if we look closer, the rhythm of mind seems itself to be but an extension of that of matter. Organisms, in their reproduction, pass through the most curious seminal and embryonic phases, in which nothing human appears; essences seem to descend on things like doves out of the blue. But they have their periods, conditions, and fatal exits: they compose the forms of organic behaviour, or enacted intelligence, observable in the world. Enacted intelligence, observable sensibility, discoverable languages and works of art, though they are understood to express feeling, contain no feeling in their recognisable structure: all the essences which they can possibly embody, however subtle, prolonged, or interwoven, are essences embodied in matter; they are complexities in the one flux of events in space and time which is called nature. They are all open to scientific discovery and measure, being intrinsically dated, localised, and traceable in their genesis and effects within the material sphere.

I have mentioned feeling, supposed to be expressed in some of these observable facts; and although I have not mentioned it, there is implied throughout a transcendental observer, a spirit to whom these essences are evident and who takes note of their embodiment, position, and physical inter-relation. The natural philosopher may well protest that no feeling and no spirit is discernible in the field of his observation; and how should they be discernible there, when that is not their place nor their mode of being?   Nevertheless, he is reckoning without his host and forgetting his own existence, in so far as all that he recognises, including his own body, is from time to time focussed and actually present to him in the light of spirit; a fact patent to reflection and recorded perpetually in any honest confession or bit of autobiography, such as human discourse and conversation are chiefly composed of.   Remove this pedestal and the whole conception of nature has nothing to stand on, no means of entering into the moral world, no claim upon the living philosopher. He is a discoursing spirit by nature and a discoverer of this world only by accident, in that this world forces itself at present on his attention and belief.   Until, therefore, he finds a means of integrating somehow his spiritual being with the realm of matter, there can be no solidity in his doctrine; for all knowledge of the world, when he is collected and self-conscious, will seem to him mere babble; and at the same time he will marvel, and even tremble, at the incredible tenuity of his actual being.   He has but to shut his eyes for all that painted world to vanish; he has but to arrest the inner rumble of words for his memory and life to become a forgotten story; he has but to fall asleep for the lever of reason to lose its fulcrum altogether, and the whole argument to lapse.   We may insist that his extinction makes no difference to the realm of essence and little difference to the universe; but this very fact, since this extinction makes all the difference to him,

*Life, besides being a form of behaviour, kindles an inner light called spirit.*

establishes the ineradicable diversity between his spirit on the one hand and the universe with the realm of essence on the other.

There is in fact another way altogether, besides embodiment in matter, by which essences may be exemplified: they may be imagined. Even those which are embodied passively or for- *Unembodied essences* mally in things, if any one is ever to see or *may appear to spirit.* to attribute them, must also (perhaps at quite a different time) be imagined, felt, conceived, contemplated, or somehow directly revealed to spirit. This presence of essences occasionally to imagination was very accurately called by the Scholastics their *objective* being, contrasted with the intrinsic or logical being which they had in themselves, and with the formal embodiment which they might have in things; but in the utter confusion of modern philosophy, substances being denied in one breath and imagination in the next, " the objective " has come to mean that which is independent of intent or attention fixed upon it; which is precisely what *the objective* can never be. It is indeed the intuition of essences in their own category, when the things that may embody them are absent or non-existent, that makes up the essence of spirit, in its various forms of feeling, sense, thought, memory, or knowledge. Spirit is the actuality of the unsubstantial.

It belongs to the nature of spirit to be cognitive; for even when intuition is pure and unmixed with intent, so that there is no claim to transitive *Essence of* knowledge, no positing of facts, intuition *spirit.* must reveal an object other than its own spiritual being and activity. The intrinsic action of spirit, like that of existence (of which spirit is a special instance), cannot be itself an object of intuition: it can be exemplified only by being enacted and realised by a transition in neither term of which it could be realised separately. If spirit were ever suspended, if it ceased to live, to drink

K

in and to peruse its object, it would have literally
lost itself in that object; there would be no spirit, no
intuition, any longer, but only some essence; and
this essence for its part would no longer have any
adventitious prominence in the realm of essence;
no emphasis or actuality would fall upon it; and no
instance of it would have occurred. It is the act of
attention, synthesis, and apprehension, performed by
the psyche animating some animal, that lends to any
essence its *objective* actuality, or ideal presence; and in
so doing, and inseparably, the same act embodies and
exemplifies the essence of spirit in a particular instance.

There are accordingly two disparate essences
exemplified in every instance of spirit; one is the
essence of spirit, exemplified *formally* and embodied
in the event or fact that at such a moment such an
animal has such a feeling; the other is the essence then
revealed to that animal, and realised *objectively* or
imaginatively in his intuition. The character of this
given essence serves to distinguish morally this phase
of spirit from other possible phases. Any essence whatever, if the psyche at work has the requisite energy and
scope, may appear in intuition; even the essences of
existence and of spirit may be defined in reflection, as
I have been endeavouring to define them here; but
nothing follows as to the truth or relevance to existence
of any such visionary term; if these essences are
embodied in nature, it is because nature of her own will
embodies them in their natural places, not because I
here, and at this remove, define them in my thought.
They are by no means embodied formally in the
thought that conceives them, so as to be predicable of
this thought: my idea of God is not God, and does not
bring God into existence on its precise model; nor does
my idea of matter perform a corresponding miracle.
My ideas merely take their places among ideas, as
being images or hypotheses of a certain quality, which

any one else, if he can and will, is at liberty to conceive also; it is the occasions on which they arise, their
several organs in nature, that will distinguish their
instances historically, as well as bring them into
existence. Thus my thoughts in this book are distinguished physically, as events in the world, by belonging to my person and buzzing in my brain at the dates
and places where I rehearse them; but the same
thoughts, as essences then conceived by me, are distinguished morally by their scope and subject-matter;
eternal essences having eternal relations of contrast
or affinity with the other essences which employ my
thoughts or those of other philosophers, and beyond
that to all other essences that might be instead the
theme of any discourse.

This diversity of status between an essence embodied
and the same essence conceived remains complete even
when in its two disparate instances the Moral
essence is identical; but this is not normally essences
the case. The essences embodied even in can be
realised only the human body and total human career in spirit.
are not such as human imagination can easily conceive;
and the essences embodied in the depths and unattainable dimensions of nature escape us altogether.
On the other hand, the æsthetic and sentimental
essences which fill human discourse are often, by their
very nature, incapable of passive embodiment: they
*cannot* be true, save in the historical sense that it may
be true that some one has entertained them. So, for
instance, any quality or intensity of pain; such an
essence can be exemplified only spiritually, never
materially; its instances must be feelings. No cata-
clysm of nature, however disruptive, can ever embody
evil. Evil can be realised there only if, in virtue of a
previous organic harmony, a spirit was there incarnate,
in which the disruption could generate the intuition of
a hated change.

The same originality of spirit appears in the normal perspectives of memory and history, even when, conventionally speaking, they are true enough. My knowledge of Julius Cæsar obviously differs in date from its object; but it differs from it avowedly also in essence, since I cannot pretend to know the whole truth of Julius Cæsar, nor any part of it with complete accuracy. The most scrupulous and exhaustive historian would be satisfied with recovering a few salient particulars, revivifying these in his own fancy—that of a modern—and surrounding them with comparisons, judgements, and emotions adventitious to the inner being of Julius Cæsar and of his age. History is a poetic art; the Muse, Clio, must inspire it; and the existing correlate or controlling cause of the historian's thoughts, even when they are true, is not the object described, Cæsar, but the historian's person, his documents, studies, passions, and abilities.

*So, too, all human perspectives of nature and history.*

Mind accordingly comes to enrich the essence of the world, not to reproduce it. Condensation, expression, comparison, are also enrichments; it is not so much by repeating some literal aspect of something remote that this remote thing can be called to mind, as rather by modifying the present in deference and with reference to it; for instance, by giving it a new name or a new tragic or pictorial embodiment. The living poet and his contemporary world, in evoking this new essence, grow sensitive to that remote object, and truly intend, salute, and describe it. This they may do, because description, no less than intent or homage, are relative: the attitude and contribution of the observer are integral to it. Material, even if subtle, influences, descending from that object have stimulated him to this fresh conception; and the conception will be just and true in so far as, in the language native to this

*Spirit is nature's comment on herself, concise and emotional.*

later and living world, it expresses that influence
adequately in its present ramifications; for new state-
ments about a thing may be perfectly true, if they are
made from new points of comparison. Thought is
normally relative, expressing relations that accrue with
time; it may occasionally include a rapt imaginative
reproduction of something distant, though hardly to a
great extent or to much purpose.

Reproduction, again, is not the normal relation
between essences embodied in matter and those
revealed to spirit. Where this relation seems to obtain,
as between an architect's first idea and the building that afterwards realises it, the echo or fulfilment
really belongs to the same realm—imagination—as
the original conception. That which resembles the
visionary project, and repeats it, is not the material
house—which is a mass of whirling atoms, or invisible
energy, or something no less recondite—but simply the
*aspect* which this house presents to the architect's own
eye, or to that of a man like him. In registering such
similarities between images he has not issued from the
realm of spirit. So the reputed likeness of images
discoverable in the retina, or in a photographic plate,
to segments of the originals in nature, is a likeness
between the essence revealed to a living spirit on one
occasion and that revealed to it on another. There
is no probable or discoverable likeness between the
material composition of an eye, of a country side,
and of a sensitized plate. A living psyche must
react upon these divers substances before the actual
vision arises in any of the three cases; that three
so dissimilar substances should be able to occasion
a similar image, only proves that relatively to the
organ of sense affected they serve the same purpose
and offer an equivalent stimulus; as a gramophone,
although materially so unlike a band of rapturous
and sweating musicians, may serve the same purpose

to the ear and may offer, up to a certain point, an equivalent stimulus.

Shall we say that the exemplifications of essence in nature and in thought, although composed of very unlike forms, yet flow in parallel streams? If by parallel we understand simply not intermingled I should answer, Yes; but if by parallel we understand running side by side all the way and corresponding throughout, I should say, No. For it is contrary to the nature of spirit to arise in dead or inorganic things; and where it arises, its vistas radiate from that point, according to the material tensions present in it, forward and back along the stream of material events, and tangentially into all sorts of supervening images and rhymes. Spirit is what is called epi-phenomenal, although this word is very ill-chosen, since neither substance nor spirit is phenomenal; but the essences embodied in matter and those revealed to intuition are indeed deployed in two different media: the spiritual perspective being at each point dependent for its existence and its character upon the balance and movement of the vital process beneath. But these spiritual perspectives are called forth only occasionally, as matter rolls on; and they open out at right angles, to any distance, into the realms of truth and of essence. There are not, then, two parallel streams, but rather one stream which, in slipping over certain rocks or dropping into certain pools, begins to babble a wanton music; not thereby losing any part of its substance or changing its course, but unawares enriching the world with a new beauty. Feeling, intuition, prophetic and synthetic intelligence, are spiritual facts utterly alien to the pedestrian flux of the materially successive. They, too, are transitory, subsisting only so long as the material foci in which they are collected remain in being; but spirit, though the occasions on which it

*It is occasional, symbolic, and made in view of eternity.*

arises are material, is itself an imponderable and invisible fact; and although its interests are borrowed from the impulses and contacts of animal life, the terms in which it expresses those interests are original and poetic; and by translating nature into those terms it paints, as it were, her immortal portrait.

Which of the essences conceived by the human mind, if any, may be credited with being the absolute and intrinsic essences of the natural world, is a question to be left to the judgement and modesty of natural philosophers; I may say something about it on another occasion, in so far as the matter interests a moralist or can fall within his competence. Here I will only note that while such coincidence is possible, all essences whatsoever being open to potential intuition, every presumption is against it. Nature, if nature exists at all, is not a hypostasis of essences defined in human discourse; she is the matrix, incalculably ancient and vast, of human nature and human ideas, ideas which by their origin and their function express the sensibility and reactions of the human organism, and nothing else. To suppose that these ideas reproduce and literally define the intrinsic essence of nature is accordingly an illusion: excusable because inevitable in an animal at once active and ignorant; yet such, when maintained doggedly, as to excite inextinguishable laughter in the immortal gods.

*Conception of facts is never literal or adequate.*

But let us suppose that, by a singular miracle, human experience were clairvoyant, and assigned to all parts of nature, in so far as they were encountered materially, their intrinsic essences. It would follow that whenever the mind conceived them, the essences of things would be exemplified twice over: once formally in the flux of matter and again imaginatively in that of mind. The stream of existence would " bifur-

*Alleged introjection or bifurcation consequent on a false projection of appearances.*

cate ", and the two currents, strangely diverse in substance but strangely similar in form, would flow side
by side mirroring one another.  Or if it were found
impossible, as it would be, to regard all given essences
as embodied in natural things, first illusions, then
secondary qualities, and finally primary qualities, would
have to be " introjected" and sucked in into the mental
sphere;   the natural world would have become a
nonentity, and the result would be idealism.  All this
confusion comes of originally supposing that things
are graphically copied in sense, and nature in science;
a belief founded on the projection of the essences given
to spirit, as if the world had been created and were
now deployed on the model of human ideas.  But the
essences given to spirit are forms of imagination and
thought: they never were and never will be the essences
of things;  and it is only by poetic licence and conventional symbolism that we are compelled to clothe things
in the garb of our sensations and rhetoric.  Introjection
is therefore only the counterpart of a false earlier
projection, and bifurcation the inevitable consequence
of a pictorial physics.  Nature, let me repeat, is not
a visual image hypostatised :  she has embodied, from
indefinite past time, whatever essences she has embodied without asking our leave or conforming before-
hand (as philosophers seem to expect) to the economy
and logic of our thoughts.  These thoughts and
images of ours, with their economy, are not irrelevant
to nature, since she produces them at stated junctures;
our imagination and logic, as far as they go, are her
own logic and imagination, by which here, at least,
she finds it possible to possess and to celebrate herself
spiritually;  they are therefore true enough, and a
different logic or a different imagination would probably be no truer.  They have the value of signs and
are felt to have it;  because the spirit which evokes
them is incarnate, with transitive and not contem-

plative interests predominant in it, so that it takes all its visions, when it can, for omens of collateral powers.

By the birth of spirit nature is certainly complicated and rendered heteroclite, as animal life is later by the birth of language; but spirit can never contain any portion, not to say the whole, of the material flux that generates it. This new form of existence is immaterial, synthetic, cognitive, emotional; and any of the feelings or intuitions which compose it, when they contain a vista, contain it spiritually only, focussed and seen, not enacted piecemeal and irrevocably self - substitutive, as an actual flux must be. For the fountain of conception is internal, it is the heart; and its deliverances, being fundamentally exclamatory, pictorial, and intellectually creative, can be brought round only poetically to describe the profound dynamic structure and order of things.

*Science, no less than theology, is a form of discourse.*

# CHAPTER X

## ESSENCES ALL PRIMARY

COMPLEX essences, as we have seen, are not compounded: this is one of the most fruitful reflections which speculation about essence can suggest. It can cure us of the most stubborn prejudices in physics; it can show us the vanity of any psychologism, mental chemistry, or attempt to generate ideas out of ideas; and it can help us to place the realm of essence where it belongs at an infinite remove from the accidents of any evolving world or any intellectual or moral scale.

In the material sphere it is common for complex things, such as plants, to be formed out of others, such as seeds, earth, sunshine, and water, which to human apprehension are more simple. The arts visibly continue this process of construction; an architect, for instance, deliberately causes various materials to be collected and built into his edifice; and the finished building is evidently an assemblage of substances and patterns, each of which was known first in isolation, and now contributes, mechanically or æsthetically, to a result which, since the architect half-intended, half-desired, and half-directed it, seems to him an achievement. At the same time the very certainty that he has selected these elements and combined them, and that they undoubtedly conspire more or less obviously to

*In material compounds the essence of the whole is not compounded of the essences of the parts.*

produce the result, may cause him some disappointment and, if he is metaphysically inclined, some perplexity; for many of those elements, æsthetically considered, have disappeared or have changed their character; and even the total effect, or actual uses, of the structure, in carrying out approximately his material specifications, are unprecedented, and fall together otherwise than he expected. Indeed, the poverty of the result, artistic and moral, may be out of all proportion to the richness of detail and the careful intentions which occupied him in making the plans. The angels that watched his labour will not revisit the finished work; the essence of the whole is not compounded of the essences of the parts, but is a new essence, a summary unity, perhaps simpler, and at any rate original.

A thorough appreciation of this point would save philosophers from many a false assumption and insoluble problem. Things are never compounded of their qualities, but of their substances. If the composite thing retains vestiges of the original qualities of the parts, this is due to an imperfect fusion of the materials, such that each part remains a separate fact, still separately observable; this happens in discursive painting or description of mere aggregates, never in living intuition or in theoretic insight. Again, even when the compound is single and new, the effect of it on some organ blunt to this new order of essences may be very like the effect of one or other of the original objects; as when we complain how monotonous and equivalent things or persons are in this world, in spite of their newness. It follows that any degree of composition in a thing may go with a perfect simplicity in its total essence, be this essence formal or specious; nor can this resulting essence have been native to any of the components. It has been embodied, or has appeared (as the case may be) by a formal necessity or by a natural mutation, upon the juxtaposition of those elements. So a spark may result from the friction of two bodies, who knows how complex; a pure pain may result from an elaborate disorder; a rounded blue sky may result from a flat sea of refracting atoms caught in an earthly eye. The living transcript of facts into sensations, without ceasing to be a mystery (as all existence must be) thus ceases to seem an anomaly; for if anything new was ever to arise or to be revealed to sense, it *had* to assume an essence not the essence of its compound conditions; and it simply remains for observation to specify, when it can, what the normal transformations are for the time being in our parts of the universe.

*When the material complex is an animal reaction, the specious essence evoked in sense is single and novel.*

There is a stock objection to materialism that looks very foolish when seen in the light of these essential necessities. Matter, it is said, cannot explain the origin of life, of consciousness, or of morals. Matter here means the *essence* which some philosopher attributes, or is alleged to attribute, to matter; this essence has probably suggested itself to the philosopher's imagination after much consideration of the ways of nature; it is a simple, perhaps a merely mathematical term. Now no essence can be the origin of anything: not even of another essence, much less of any fact. But the forms which nature wears could not be successive, or be embodied anywhere, if matter did not assume, connect, and exchange them. Of course this real matter, coming down through the ages, and falling into all these forms, is not anybody's *idea* of matter: its intrinsic essence is unknown, and if we prefer for that reason to call it by another name, we are at liberty to do so, provided we honestly attribute to it, under that sweeter name, all the relations and functions by which the existence of matter has become certain to common sense, and has been assumed by science and

*A vain objection to materialism.*

the arts, since the beginning of history.  The essence
which any man attributes to matter expresses his own
experience much better than it does the nature of
matter itself; but it will be a true idea, as a sensation or
a maxim may be true, if it exactly reports some circumstance or relation or specious quality which it interests
us to discover in that province of nature.  The point
that interests us in practical science and art is the
method of genesis in things, which determines the
successive embodiment of essences in them, their
quantity and distribution.  The essences distinguish
the occasions, but the movement of matter produces them in their places, and makes those essences
relevant to existence at all.  The incapacity of the
materialist to deduce logically from the terms of his
theory—such as extension, atoms, electric charges,
energy, or what not—the other variegated terms in
which our senses or imagination may picture the world,
is therefore a matter of course; far from being a defect,
this is a sign that his theory is not merely verbal but
may have penetrated beneath the confused surface of
events and partly traced their dynamic thread; whereas
a pictorial physics that should literally reproduce everything just as it appears would be entirely unintelligent
and perfectly useless.

There is a more speculative prejudice which should
also vanish before the equal primacy of all essences: it
is the feeling that complexity, beyond a $_{\text{In the realm}}$
certain point, is something difficult, unlikely, $_{\text{of essence}}$
and incredible.  This feeling is human, too $_{\text{the true has}}^{\text{no priority}}$
human;  it expresses our scepticism or $_{\text{over the}}$
amusement or despair before any object that $_{\text{false, nor}}^{\text{the natural}}$
stretches too much our powers of intuition. $_{\text{over the}}$
It is relative to the human scale, and has no $_{\text{unnatural.}}$
meaning in the field of being as a whole.  The measure
of complexity or of unity that best suits the human
mind is itself variable; but wherever it may be fixed, it

will mark one degree in an infinite series of proportions, each neither more nor less central or proper than any other degree. Even nature seems to be full of a vastness and a minuteness that baffle us, yet are her homeliest accidents; and disproportionate as her scale may be to our fancy, she after all contains us and this fancy of ours; and at bottom she may be composed in a fashion relatively sympathetic to our categories of thought, for instance, atomically, monotonously, or subject to calculation; so that to speak of composition, elaboration, and a precarious evolved complexity, may not be meaningless in respect to natural things. Even size, childish as the notion seems, might have a natural measure: for instance, if the more atoms a thing contained the larger it should be said to be, or if the organising forces emanating from one nucleus had a greater scope than those emanating from another, so that the smaller organism might be enveloped in the larger and be a part of it. If a thing is finite either inwards or outwards, forward or back, a scale may be fixed by which it may be internally measured. But in the realm of essence all such foothold fails for human prerogative. Here every degree of complexity is as calmly enthroned as every other: none is more primitive or natural or safe than the rest, since all are necessary and all eternal. The most agitated *Paradiso* ever painted by Tintoretto, the most insane *Walpurgisnachtstraum*, is as elementary and fundamental an essence as the number one or the straight line. The realm of essence never was formed; there are no seeds or accretions in it; and we may as legitimately imagine the simple, the monotonous, or the chaotic to be derogations from some organic form, as this organic form to be a composition out of those elements. Existence, that everlasting Penelope, may sometimes embroider and sometimes undo; but all the mornings and all the evenings are one eternity, in which the finished work and the ultimate elements are equally present.

Nor is this parity of all essences confined to those which may figure in the evolution of a single world, from its atoms to the idea of its total system, seen under the form of eternity: the parity extends to the unused essences as well. Existence, infinite as it may be in some direc- tions and by a perpetual budding, is narrowly hedged in at every step; it is all bias and exclusions. Not so the depths of pure Being: there all is simultaneous, nothing forbidden, nothing pre-eminent. The home- lessness or even terror which sometimes assaults the mind at the thought of so many stars and planets, so many animals and cross-purposes even on earth, is redoubled when we consider the truly remorseless infinity of essence. It contains with perfect placidity, and without begging leave either of God or man, everything whatsoever. The selections which nature may make out of that manifold store, whether she picks a simple thing out first or a complex thing first (and who shall say which she picks out first, if she has been picking them out alternately for ever?), establish no essential priority among them. It is as easy for Being to be great as to be little: no effort is concerned, no probability; all great things and all little things are equally integral to the infinite.

It follows that all psychologisms, all attempts to analyse given essences into original elements or to assign to them a history or a meaning, are so many materialisms in disguise. Those elements are not elements of the given essence, but are other whole essences which might have been given when the material situation was different. Such history is not the history of these ideas (which have no history) but of the natural course of events which led up to the moment which begat these ideas; a course of

Nor the existent over the non-existent.

Essences have no family tree.

events which, at various points, may have begotten other ideas introducing those now alive, and having (for the best of reasons) a family likeness to them. Finally those meanings are not proper to those essences (which are what they are and have no further meaning) but express the residual pregnancy of the mind, tempted to wander dramatically, and to trace the material agencies, past or future, which may have flowed into or may flow out of the present event, in which now, like bursting rockets, these essences shine forth. Such past and future events will bear names, and will be indicated by imaginary terms which are themselves essences; but the whole force of the felt derivation will come, not from these terms or names, but from an impulse sweeping through them, rehearsed in discourse, and covering the unspecified flux of material forces actually carrying events forward from phase to phase. If the reader will recall the method of Hegel or that of Taine, he will understand what I mean: a set of brilliant dramatic sketches or notes of moral attitudes, strung together so as to suggest a voluminous current of evolution carrying these various spiritual moments on the crest of its waves. It is a material movement sketched by romantic suggestion and wrapped in moralistic eloquence or even in prophecy.

The only veritable idealism is Platonic: it sees in essences the essences themselves, self-enclosed and insulated, ultimate and eternal. The occasions on which they are manifested may be traced according to the physics or theology in vogue: that temporal underpinning cannot change their intrinsic nature. And as the means of purifying and coming truly to possess an essence is simply to contemplate it, so the means of conceiving the essences given elsewhere, for instance in the feelings and thoughts of other men, is poetic imagination, dramatic sympathy. Shakespeare is your only psychologist: the others are

Their only genealogy is that of their occasions.

physiologists or external observers who entangle their
poetic science in a net of scholastic fictions. The
mechanism of life being very obscure and remote from
gross observation, it is inevitable that it should be
adumbrated at first in fables and metaphors. When
the notion of matter is crude and pictorial, there is need
of piecing it out with crude and pictorial notions of
souls, psychic mechanisms, laws of association, moral
dialectic, and blasts of supernatural influence. These
are only other names for veritable matter and its secret
work; but they point to facts which science may over-
look, if it has grown up in the practice of mechanical
arts. Maturity, in the rhetorical school of physics,
will render these myths more and more harmless and
transparent, as it will all other forms of rhetoric; while
maturity in the scientific school, if it is ever attained,
will reduce those pictorial models more frankly to
symbols, and the field of science to the field of action.
But it is not the reform of science that interests me
here; I am concerned to rescue from oblivion one of
those preliminary facts which the science of things
external ignores, although it is the breath of its nostrils:
I mean intuition, with the inevitable unity and originality of the essence which that intuition defines from
moment to moment.

There is no reason to suppose that nature began by
being simpler than she is; we may rather suppose that
she has cycles, perhaps local cycles, of relative **Essences**
complication with intervals of dissolution or **given on**
chaos. And the beginnings of intuition can **complex occasions**
be reasonably looked for only at the height, **may be**
or near the height, of this complication; **simple and must be**
intuition presupposes reactive adjustment, **unitary.**
psychic inertia or propulsion, and therefore an elaborate hereditary life such as only a most delicately-
balanced cosmos could contain. Yet though begotten
and nurtured in the lap of complexity, intuition opens

L

its childish eyes upon blank light; experience does
begin with the simple, although nature does not.   The
intuition of a simple essence is called a feeling; and the
essence given in a primitive feeling is likely to be some
truly simple, quite stupid, essence, such as sheer intensity.   This intensity, when there is some concomitant
motion excited in the animal, may seem vaguely to have
a seat and to lie in some quarter; and it may be coloured
with an incipient tint of uneasiness or of contentment.
Above all, this intensity will be felt to wax and wane;
it comes as a waxing, an interruption to repose; and
the interruption over or gulped down, repose comes
slowly back.   So at least I conceive it: nature may
have many different ways of calling forth intuition,
here stealthily, there perhaps suddenly with a flare of
trumpets, and with a consciousness of having always
existed and of being omniscient.   Suffice it that this
first revelation, whether to worm or god, is a specious
thing, having a specious unity, and a precise specious
character; the vagueness or abstractness imputed to it,
when compared with the supposed material circumstances, are its very definition and familiar aspect
taken in itself.   It may be a whiff of emotion; it may
be a perception; it may be a moral sentiment redolent
of a thousand high thoughts and profound tragedies:
in each case it will be a complete apparition, born at
that moment and dying with it.   The onlooker, if
informed of its existence, may understand its origin,
its truth or falsity, its promise for the future; these are
relations external to it, physical or historical.   They
can be disclosed only when all the postulates of physics,
which are those of action, have been made by the
discursive intellect in the service of animal faith.   In
itself the given essence signifies only that which it is;
its inner perspectives, if any, are of its essence; such
reports or imaginations of things beyond as may trouble
it are elements in its being.   It is the deliverance of a

dream: the remote exists in it only as a part of the immediate. There is no complexity and no length of evolution which the immediate may not synthesise in one picture and possess in its essence. If experience in the child begins with the simple, in the wise man it begins with the complex; and his wisdom need not trouble to banish that complexity and revert to the simple, if it can learn to envisage the complex as a pure essence, in its harmless immediacy. Whether his spirit rests on a simple or a complex essence will make no difference to the purity of his contemplation, but will turn on his mood or the accidents of his life and education—things irrelevant to spiritual insight.

When I say that in a given essence all its parts are given, is not this an enormous exaggeration? It would be, if I meant the material or natural parts of an existing object; these would not only be impossible to assemble into any human view, but would be impossible to define or distinguish individually; for the structure of things is fluid, their composition perhaps infinite inwards, and their relations outwards certainly inexhaustible. But I am speaking of the features actually composing a given essence, and these by definition are all there. They are not, and can never be, anywhere else; for they are merely the features found as they are found, and where they are found, possessing the precise degree of definition, separation, and connection which they have in that living moment. As to be a living act of spirit is the nature of intuition, so to be an individual unity is the nature of essence.

Let me give three familiar illustrations of this: one drawn from emotion, one from perception, and one from imagination.

Suppose that in a Spanish town I come upon an apparently blind old beggar sitting against a wall, thrumming his feeble guitar, and uttering an occasional hoarse wail by way of singing. It is a sight which I have passed a hundred times unnoticed; but now suddenly I am arrested and seized with a voluminous unreasoning sentiment—call it pity, for want of a better name. An analytic psychologist (I myself, perhaps, in that capacity) might regard my absurd feeling as a compound of the sordid aspect of this beggar and of some obscure bodily sensation in myself, due to lassitude or bile, to a disturbing letter received in the morning, or to the general habit of expecting too little and remembering too much; or if the psychologist was a Freudian, he might invoke some suppressed impression received at the most important period of life, before the age of two. But since that supposed impression is forgotten and those alleged causes are hypothetical, they are no part of what I feel now. What I feel is simply, as Othello says, "the pity of it". And if I stop to decipher what this *it* contains, I may no doubt be led, beyond my first feeling, to various images and romantic perspectives. My fancy might soon be ranging over my whole universe of discourse, over antiquity, over recent wars, over so many things ending in smoke; and my discursive imagery would terminate in dreary cold facts, the prose of history, from which my emotion would have wholly faded. The pity is not for them: it is not for the old man, perhaps a fraud and a dirty miser; it is pity simply, the pity of existence, suffusing, arresting, rendering visionary the spectacle of the moment and spreading blindly outwards, like a light in the dark, towards objects which it does not avail to render distinguishable. There is, then, in this emotion, no composition. There is pregnancy, a quality having affinity with certain ulterior things rather than with others; but these things are not given; they are not needed in the emotion, which arises absolutely in its full quality and in its strong simplicity. My life might have begun and ended there. Nothing is too

*Illustrations: First, the emotion of pity.*

complex to be primitive; nothing is too simple to stand alone.

Suppose now that I turn through the town gates and suddenly see a broad valley spread out before me with the purple sierra in the distance beyond. Second, the This expanse, this vastness, fills my intuition; perception also, perhaps, some sense of the deeper breath of distance. which I draw as if my breast expanded in sympathy with the rounded heavens. Here the psychologist intervening may demur, and say that I cannot see depth, because depth is a straight line terminating in the eye, along which it is impossible for the eye to travel. Distance, he will assert, must be conveyed to me through a muscular sense and the suggestion of motion; and my perception of the landscape must be compounded of a flat picture in the retina *plus* sensations in the muscles of the eye or (as I was innocently confessing) elsewhere in the body, conveying to me the suggestion of a great opportunity to move.

It is very true that pictorial space, or the specious essence of extension, appears in intuition to animals capable of locomotion, whose attention has a forward direction—that of action—so that they are capable of feeling the difference between right and left, up and down, forward and back, here and there. All the internal and external organs of their bodies are engaged in these movements, and it is fair to suppose that they all contribute something to the picture of space which, in living, dominates their spirits. But this picture is not, in itself, laid out in three dimensions. Sensible These are first discriminated by the geometry space is of builders in their material blocks and stones, a single and are specified in their working drawings essence. and calculations. To attempt to piece together pictorial space out of imaginary earlier intuitions of dismembered geometrical elements would be the height of artifice. The third dimension does not need to be added to the

other two, because the other two never appear without
it.  Breathing, stifling, writhing, and running are not
felt, or seen, to occur in flatland before they are felt
and seen to occur in space.  Perhaps, since the possibilities of pure intuition are infinite, some paralytic
geometer might see a plane in two dimensions at no
distance and in no direction from himself—the pure
essence of flatness lying nowhere or lying just there,
in its own flat world; and nothing militates against
the possibility of conceiving a mathematical plane, if
circumstances lead some rapt spirit to lose itself in that
essence.  But such an essence would be no part of the
specious essence of extension as given to ordinary
mortals: it would not even be, in any literal sense, an
abstraction from the latter, but an essence of a different
kind (as algebraic essences are different from geometrical, or writing from speech); and nevertheless
it might serve to describe in part the same material
objects.  A plane actually imagined is a feature in
pictorial space, not an antecedent to it;  the plane is
viewed from a point outside and in front of it;  its
length and breadth are relative to the distance at which
it lies.  Animals surely begin by seeing moving objects
in a particular quarter beyond themselves, away from
the occupied centre of their own bodies;  else seeing
would not be looking, as it is in the play of action.

Even if we suppose that originally the intuition of
extension was not a perception but only a diffuse
All genetic  feeling without indicative force, this felt
psychology  extension would be spread in all directions,
is a dis-
guised  spherical and roomy, and by no means a
materialism. surface without space before and behind it.
For the analysis of such essences given in intuition,
which is a literary task, all physiological or metaphysical
hypotheses are worse than useless; they are sophistical
and blinding, and tend only to falsify the honest face of
experience.  The question whether I see distance is a

question not for science but for me.  If I see distance
I see it;  if I infer it—as when I ask myself how far a
distant object may be—I infer it;  but the contention
that when I see it I must nevertheless be inferring it, is
impertinent.  From what should I infer it, when the
result of the supposed inference is the only essence
before me?  Nothing is present to the spirit at any
time but what is then present to it;  this cannot be in
the least altered by the fact that other things may have
been present to it, or to other spirits, at other times.
These other moments will have, no doubt, an equal
importance to themselves;  and memory or theory,
surveying them in their imagined order, may see a
plot or development in them, which may seem more
interesting than any of them in isolation;  but this
history or plot exists for the spirit only in that contemplative or retrospective moment in which, as at the end
of a Greek tragedy, it is summed up and proclaimed.
Such a plot is a perspective in the imagination, a poetic
or philosophic idea, itself a surface view of surfaces;
the causes of all these incidents, of their existence as
well as their sequence, lie far beneath.  Ideas are not
material things, or tribes of animals, though idealists
might seem to think so;  in tracing their genesis or
evolution through the world, it is the movement of the
world, of the conditions and causes of those ideas, that
we are tracing under their name.  An intuition is like
a flame; if the substance that fed it can continue to feed
it, or can kindle it again, it may endure or revive, in the
midst of such other intuitions as the flux of life may
involve.  Discourse thus proceeds in a connected but
spasmodic manner, expressing at each moment the
cumulative energies, habits, and impulses of the
psyche, herself a mode or cycle of physical events; but
the phases of spirit, the actual intuitions and emotions
which diversify experience, are as little capable of
adding themselves up as the kisses of yesterday are

of building nests in the air and hatching the kisses of
to-morrow.

Suppose, finally, a Chinaman at the Louvre invited
to admire the Venus of Milo.  The admiration expected
Third, the sense of beauty. of him is to be a spiritual emotion, an actual
flight or transport into a fresh region of
the beautiful.  It will not do if intellectually
he is able to recognise the master-lines of the statue,
although broken or because broken;  nor if he can
recall the place which our historians of art may assign
to such a theme in the development of sculpture.  I
will assume that he is a man of cultivated taste, accustomed to the arts of his own country, so full of delicate
ministrations to the senses and so flattering to the
ironies, perhaps to the cruelties, of the mind.  He will
relegate to their place the keys to universal history
offered by philosophers, and the technical devices that
may seem for the moment the whole of art to the snobs
of the studio;  and after listening to both he may continue to feel in his heart that this leaning block of
marble is blank and heavy;  that a Greek goddess is
but a stalwart washer-woman;  and that such monu-
mental designs are thick, vacant, chalky, clumsy, and
rude.  He will remain cold, because he will miss here
the things which in his case can work the miracle and
entrance the mind: things minute, ornate, suave, parti-
coloured, fragrant, incidental.

The sense of beauty is not a feeling separable from
some intuition of form;  on the other hand, it is a feeling,
The sources and their composition belong to the material life of the psyche. not a verbal or intellectual judgement.  It
arises by the convergence in the psyche of
many assaults and many reactions, from far
and near.  Some of these influences may
come from the region which the æsthetes of
the last generation denounced as morality,
or from that which the æsthetes of to-day denounce as
literature;  some may come from erotic sensibility,

from familiarity, from lucidity, from harmony with other esteemed things. The Venus of Milo will not seem beautiful, in any deep sense, to any one incapable of feeling the luminous scorn, the victorious perfection, of the Greek immortals. But all this composition, though we may give moral names to its elements, occurs underground: it is physical and merely preliminary to the beauty realised in intuition. This realised beauty is not compounded of those miscellaneous extinct impressions: it could certainly not be bred in a soil which these impressions had not raked and watered, but it is a fresh flower, with its own form, its own scent, and its own naughtiness. For this reason too it cannot be preserved mummified in any external object; it can belong to things only by being attributed to them by some living soul. Those who insist that the marble Venus must be either beautiful or ugly in itself, apart from all Greeks and Chinamen, are allowing a grammatical form of judgement to mislead them about the subtler ways in which essences may be manifested in the world. Not the marble which a man without any sense of beauty might see, is the seat of beauty; the contrary quality may be as truly attributed to it. The only Venus which is inalienably beautiful is the divine essence revealed to the lover as he gazes, perhaps never to be revealed to another man, nor revealed to himself again. In this manifest goddess (for so the gods were originally revealed) her beauty is indeed intrinsic and eternal; and it is as impossible that its particular quality should be elsewhere, as that she should be without it.

The beauty felt is unprecedented, single, and revealed only to enthusiasm.

The nature of essence appears in nothing better than in the beautiful, when this is a positive presence to the spirit and not a vague title conventionally bestowed. In a form felt to be beautiful an obvious complexity composes an obvious unity: a marked intensity and individuality are seen to belong to a reality utterly immaterial and incapable of existing otherwise than speciously. This divine beauty is evident, fugitive, impalpable, and homeless in the world of material fact; yet it is unmistakably individual and sufficient unto itself, and although perhaps soon eclipsed is never really extinguished: for it visits time, but belongs to eternity.

# CHAPTER XI

THE type of being which I call essence has long been familiar to philosophers, and it is unfamiliar to the man in the street, not because it is too remote Pure essence from him but because it is too near. I might discerned by almost say that my theory is a variant of Plato and materialised Platonism, designed to render Platonic logic by him. and morals consistent with the facts of nature. I am afraid, however, that this readjustment unhinges Platonism so completely that I have no right to call my doctrine Platonic. In the realm of essence as I conceive it, the sphere of Socratic Ideas is infinitely extended and freed from all confusion with natural forces. I am no pupil of Plato's in all that phase of his thought in which he seems to supply the lack of a cosmology by turning moral and ideal terms into supernatural powers. The supernatural is nothing but an extension of the natural into the unknown, and there is infinite room for it; but when these deeper or remoter parts of nature are described in myths evidently designed for the edification or easier government of human society, I distrust the fiction. I distrust it, I mean, as a piece of physics, or information about matters of fact; but it may be a genuine and beautiful expression of the moral experience and the moral interests which have prompted it. In this capacity even the myths and the cosmology of Plato are memorable; they become again pure essences for poetic contemplation, like the Ideas; and their moral significance helps to render them warm and interesting to a man of feeling without deceiving him about the conditions of his natural life.

In calling his Ideas ideas and his myths myths, Plato seems to acknowledge that they are, after all, nothing but essences; the power which they were represented as exercising over nature was not their chief claim to respect. Nature was a phenomenon to be superseded; the material image once shattered, the god which it represented so imperfectly would appear in his proper glory. His power was an accidental effect due to the proximity of a matter capable of reflecting his likeness, and of preserving it for a time; his intrinsic and eternal being was that of an essence. Such, I think, was the fundamental conviction of Plato, in his free moments; at least such was afterwards the experience of many a Platonising soul, in ages more religious than that of Plato.

*This materialisation only incidental.*

Without any pretence to be religious or mystical I find myself daily in that case. I cannot read a book or think of a friend or grieve or rejoice at any fresh event, without some essence rising sensibly before me, the sole actual harvest to me of that labour. At every moment the rattle of the machine of nature, and of my own engine, unless I lose the sense of it altogether, is at once revealed and hidden by some immediate essence, which it wears like a shining garment, or more often, perhaps, merely suggests to me as its meaning, its beauty, or its secret. How should spirit ever come upon anything else? Yet this trick of arresting the immediate is in one sense an interruption to life; it is proper only to poets, mystics, or epicureans; it was incompatible with the political, censorious

*Essence appears pure in poetic immediacy and disinterestedness.*

temper of a traditional Greek philosopher. Socrates
and Plato on the whole were conservative. They were
absolutely serious only in their patriotism, in their
legislative convictions, in their zeal for a well-ordered
life. The rest of their philosophy was designed to be a
safeguard or an ornament for the perfect citizen. They
were content that his mind should dwell in a castle of
words, in a mythical world no matter how fantastic, if
only his hand was strengthened thereby and his will
concentrated on maintaining intact the stone walls and
the iron laws of his city. The same sentiment is
perennial with conservatives, and would be reasonable
if any city or any morality could really be conserved;
but substance is in flux, in spite of the cries of all tragic
heroes. Myths, maintained artificially, cannot restore
morality; but a new harmony in life, defining a new
morality, will clothe itself spontaneously in some new
myth. Socrates and Plato could not revive the Greek
city which they loved, but they facilitated the triumph
of Christianity, which would have filled them with
horror. The stone walls crumbled and the air-castle
remained. Essence thus came to its own again, but
abusively, pretending to be more than essence; and
mankind has been divided ever since between the
impulse to admire the vision and the impulse to
denounce the lie.

If a philosophy like Platonism, founded on the
intuition of essences, so soon materialised them into
existences, spirits, and powers (objects of It is
belief not amenable to intuition), no wonder normally
that other systems, initially interested only overlooked
in science
in alleged facts, physical, psychological, or and experi-
theological, should have overlooked essences ence.
altogether. Not that the most distracted or dogmatic
mind ever ceases in fact to contemplate mere essences,
namely, the terms in which it frames its views, and the
emotions with which it views them; but the object it is

intent upon is always an ulterior object, an existing world, where the things and events it believes in shall stand or move in a framework of external relations.  When it calls these existences sensations, atoms, space, time, or persons, and wonders which of these names describes them best, the test does not lie in any comparison of the essences evoked by those names and the essences of the existing objects, for since these objects are removed facts their essences cannot be present to intuition.  The consequence is that even in thought the given essences lose their interest; you stop asking yourself what positive notion you have of a person or an atom, of space or of time, or of a sensation;  the choice between these notions becomes like the choice of words in a sentence, not determined so much by their intrinsic character as by the relations into which they fall and the current of intent and expectation that runs through some in one direction and through others in another.  In other words, what concerns the naturalistic philosopher in his choice of terms is the external relations which, in using them, he is led to attribute to the pressing events which they designate.  For his purposes an atom is the unit (whatever it may be) in physical transformations; a sensation is a means (no matter what) of registering a fact; a person is a centre (be it what it will) of observation or opinion.  In this way not only physics but psychology comes to disregard the actual terms in which it frames its system, and empiricism overlooks the only objects of immediate experience.

Nevertheless the bias of such an outlook exclusively towards existence is too violent not to have its nemesis. Essences neglected here will assert themselves there; they will invade and perhaps absorb the ultimate description of what is supposed to be an existing world.  Those who reject essences as terms swallow them as myths.  Descriptions of the universe, when clear, are so fantastic, so

*But, inevitably intervening, fills both with illusions.*

evidently mere essences evoked in human thought, that the very interest in existence which begat those descriptions presently disowns them, and everybody wonders how such studious and earnest men could be the dupes of their own fables.    But in reality those fables are not more fantastic than the daily aspect of the sunset or the grammar of common speech.    They are essences appearing just as immediately to the mind, only more laboured and articulate; and as symbols for the facts of nature they may be just as true.    Indeed, their immediate charm sometimes overcomes philosophers at the end of their speculation, as it overcomes artists and poets at the beginning; they see that what delights them is not a fact, not even a truth, but an absolute essence. This ultimate recognition of essence is normal in mathematics; nor can it be easily avoided in metaphysics, especially when mathematics, logic, or poetry becomes dominant there, and takes the bit in its teeth.

When Descartes, for example, identified matter with extension, he substituted essence for substance: an improvement, no doubt, for mathematical purposes, but an abdication in genuine physics, which is founded on animal faith. Substance was what Descartes meant to describe; it moved, and extension, being an essence, cannot move.    When he imagined geometrical figures, indistinguishable in scale, parts, or quality, and bounded by merely ideal lines, nevertheless moving in reference to one another, he was substituting a possible *pattern* of nature for living nature herself.    The essence in his clear and distinct intuition seemed to him fundamental and final; and so it would be to pure spirit; he forgot that a spirit cannot be born, die, or have a local habitation in the bosom of an essence.    The only substance remaining in his system—the only being self-existent in all its parts and in actual flux—was accordingly the

*Descartes, by substituting essences for substances, unintentionally left pure discourse to be the only existence.*

discourse in which the material world might appear as a picture. Descartes thus became the father of psychologism against his will; and the scientific reform which he meant to establish liberated mathematics and mechanics, but otherwise left confusion worse confounded.

It was reserved for Spinoza, still under the persuasion that he was describing substance, to conceive the realm of essence in its omnimodal immensity. Human vanities, whether in speculation or in manners, were not for him. He had a just conception of man's place in nature, and in the presence of the infinite, love cast out both fear and greed from his mind. His approach to essence is the more interesting for not being guided by any Platonic motive; as he never cultivated poetry or sentimental theology, so he might have neglected essence altogether, if he had taken it merely for what it is. All that his pious heart respected was substance—that which exerts force, works in nature, and might feed or threaten him in his contentment. In spite of his speculative scope, his wisdom was Levitical; he craved above all things to be safe and sure in his corner of the Lord's house. This safety had, as it were, two phases, or two dimensions: materially, in the lea of the tempest, the swallow might build his temporary nest; such happiness was a part of what universal nature provided; but ideally he might borrow the wings of the storm, and enjoy perfect freedom in identity with that force which in creating and destroying all things is never exhausted or defeated.

*Spinoza discerns the infinity of the realm of essence.*

It was the plethora of this passion, at once sacrificial and omnivorous, that carried Spinoza into the realm of essence, and made him gloat on its infinity. He found a cruel pleasure in asserting that every part of it existed, thereby putting to shame the conceit of mankind, and in that abasement finding a fanatical compensation for his

*His pantheist zeal leads him to hypostatise it.*

own frailty. Why, indeed, should not all essence exist? If extension be the essence of matter, every possible geometrical figure, in every possible super-position and substitution, must be equally real at every point in nature; and yet at all points pure extension, motionless and undivided, must be somehow the only reality. So in the other, the psychological, world. If thinking be the substance of all thoughts, all possible thoughts should be equally present in every act of thinking, and yet nothing in any thought should be real except the act of thinking in its purity.

This tragic contradiction—tragic because so many instincts and passions meet and destroy themselves there — comes of hypostatising essence and attempting to rationalise substance. The substance of this world (as I may have occasion to argue in its place) is no mere essence, such as extension, pure Being, or pure con-sciousness, hypostatised in its bareness: it is an exis-tential flux, of unknown extent and complexity, which when it falls into certain temporary systems which we call living bodies, kindles intuition there, and brings various essences to light, which become terms in belief and knowledge; but substance, although thus posited and symbolised by the animal mind, always remains obscure to it. How should the essences, mainly emotional and inwardly elicited, which events evoke in this or that sensitive organism, reveal substance in its inmost constitution and total extent? That substance, at this point, has produced those appearances is indeed one of its characteristics, and so much we may safely assert of it forthwith; but to legislate for substance in our private parliament, or to assert that the whole realm of essence must somewhere be reduced to act (as Spinoza supposed) is perfectly gratuitous. More-over, when the definition of the realm of essence—all distinct beings of all kinds—is turned into a definition

*The prin-ciple of existence cannot be rational.*

M

of substance, it contradicts another definition—pure Being—which Spinoza could not help regarding, with equal rashness, as the essence of substance in some deeper sense.  Natural substance must be allowed to rejoice in whatever essence it has, and to change it as often as it will, and to bring to intuition in our scattered minds such visions as it likes; and meantime, in the realm of essence, pure Being and all beings may lie eternally together like the lion and the lamb, in the peace of non-existence.  Very likely, in its chosen ways, the existing world may be infinite; but the inevitable absolute infinity of the realm of essence (a matter of definition) does not justify me in ascribing a fabulous infinity to substance.

In Leibniz (who had a wonderfully clear head) the realm of essence appears in sharp distinction from existence, under the name of " all possible worlds "; but this notion is introduced almost playfully, in the midst of a theological myth. We are invited to assist at the deliberations of the Creator when in his primeval solitude he debated which of the worlds that he could imagine might most congenially keep him company; for it was not good, he felt, for God to be alone.  Now, if we take this fable literally, the Creator already existed and was himself one of the possible worlds, and a very special one; for he possessed an intuition of the whole realm of essence, and, beneath that, a mysterious propulsive nature of his own which inclined him to create other living beings, and enabled him to distinguish a better and a worse among mere possibles. Indeed, if we remember the religious sources of this conception, which Leibniz was obliged to treat with respect, we may safely say that this gallery of possibles present to the Creator's mind is not the realm of essence at all, but an emanation of his particular existing nature; just as it is not the realm of essence

*In Leibniz it reappears both infinite and pure, but in a dubious theological context.*

in its entirety that swims before a novelist when he debates what conclusion to give to his novel; but the alternatives that suggest themselves are only a few, such as lie within his experience and conspire with his purpose and are compatible with the plot of the novel as far as it has gone. This Creator would then be a perfectly contingent existence, a particular being finding himself already at work. He could not have asked himself, before he existed, whether he would be the best possible God. The fabled problem of creation must already have been solved before it could be proposed; and a mind considering which world to choose is a world existing without ever having been chosen. The notions of the possible and the best, otherwise unintelligible, become significant in reference to the accidental potencies and preferences of that existing being. His creations, like those of any living artist, would then be naturally in his own image, and it would turn out that of all those possible worlds only the best was really possible, since a motive for creating one of the others would necessarily be wanting: the best would be simply the one which the Creator actually preferred and must have preferred unless (what is inadmissible) he did not know his own mind. I need not enter into the moral difficulties which this rigid monotheism involves; suffice it that the realm of essence has dropped out of sight, and our philosophy is reduced to an account, credible or incredible, of some natural events and some natural existences.

But perhaps we should not press in this manner words which a philosopher could only have meant figuratively. Leibniz makes some explicit reservations about time: the original solitude of God was ontological only, not historical, and time, being an integral part of creation, could not have preceded the creative act. In reality, then, this creative act would be the perpetual process of nature,

*How this might be rationalised.*

viewed under the form of eternity and represented poetically as deliberate and voluntary. If we allowed ourselves to continue this method of rationalisation, perhaps the realm of essence would come into its own again, and the mind of the Creator surveying all possible worlds would be only a dramatic metaphor for that immutable background which the realm of essence supplies for all the shifts of existence. Perhaps, too, the moral compulsion which, according to Leibniz, God was under, to distinguish and to create the best of possible worlds, might be interpreted as inverting mythically a homely truth: namely, that the best and only possible world for a creature to live in is the world that produced him. We may grumble and we may suffer, but we should not have been ourselves in any other world or nation or family; the circle of our demands and ideals is but a floating expression of the faculties which reality has fostered in us. The actual world, in type if not in detail, is therefore always such as it would be if the good to which it aspires had created it. This is the reason why at bottom most people are so well satisfied with their country and with themselves, and why existence is normally regarded as a benefit.

Leibniz could be a very great philosopher when he chose, when the press of business allowed, or when some Serene Highness commanded it; but he was a diplomatist even in philosophy, and his chief preoccupation was to reconcile powerful opinions and to recommend himself to the orthodox as well as to the competent. He could play as readily with the notion of essence as with any other notion, but his sincerity was not of that profound sort which gives to human conceptions their radical values, and his system was a masterpiece of artificiality in which nobody—not even himself—could very heartily believe.

Essence was familiar to Descartes, Spinoza, and Leibniz, because even if not scholastic themselves they were trained in the scholastic tradition, which was itself but Platonism made prosaic and Christian; but the same cannot be said of the British and German philosophers. Yet both psychology and the criticism of knowledge ought to bring essence to light, since essences are the only objects of indubitable and immediate experience. A profound confusion, however, intervened. The objects of experience were confused with experience itself, which was assumed to be self-conscious, a series of states of mind which know what they are and are what they know. Essence accordingly became a needless if not impossible conception; because the only essences that could then be found or thought of would be essences existing and knowing themselves to exist; in other words, they would not be essences but (what is a contradiction in terms) facts given in intuition. The insecurity and anarchy prevailing in these schools allow them to traverse the ground in a thousand directions without ever disengaging the radical possibilities and principles involved; for instance, they almost always combine their axiom that existence is self-conscious with a naturalistic view of the course of human experience, deployed in time and distributed among well-known persons and nations —a combination which would be impossible if either of the two views had been thoroughly analysed. The notion that existence is self-conscious, and conscious only of the state of mind which it is, excludes the possibility of any transitive knowledge or even belief, because it reduces every object, whether of intuition or intent, to the process of thinking it. The notion of a flux of experience or thought, reporting one of its parts to another of its parts, is accordingly excluded; and yet, without such naturalistic history and psychology, self-consciousness would lose all its interest, because it would be conscious of not being knowledge, but of

Modern idealism should admit only given essences, but is too distracted to rest in them.

being only the intuition of an essence devoid of meaning.

Of late, however, various judicious persons, trained in these schools, have begun to confess that conscious-ness is not aware of itself but of objects variously styled sense-data or concepts or neutral entities (neither mental not material), or simply " objects ", meaning essences present to sense or thought as opposed to the events in nature which they symbolise. But it is events, in natural knowledge, that are the true objects; and the given essences are only the terms in which those events are described. If these terms are hypostatised and set in a network of natural relations, as if they were things, the result will be a pictorial physics which may have its merits, but which is not the realm of essence; to reach the latter conception it would be necessary to remember that what is given never has any relations but those which are given with it. It is therefore always an eternal essence and never a natural fact. Natural facts are objects of intent only; and then the propriety of the names, images, categories, or other essences which we use in conceiving them becomes problematical.

*All science has need of remembering that it is only discourse.*

On the other hand, essences problematical as descriptions of facts are manifest as ideas. The more hypotheses we try, and the more alternatives we consider, whether we attain absolute truth or a sufficient symbolic truth, or no truth at all, we are still entertained by ideas which are innocent if we do not abuse them, and perhaps beautiful and significant if they express our own playful or creative impulses. Nor is this entertainment with essence a trivial bond with reality. Facts, however momentous, are transient and local, and truths, however eternal, are relative to these transient and local facts; but every essence, whether it ever have or not the adventitious dignity of a truth, is in

*And that the realm of essence is the infinite background of every-thing.*

its own right a something—a verse or a letter in that
infinite Koran sealed from all eternity in the bosom of
Allah, of which the trembling angel of life may read to
us a few Surahs.   That it should be these and not those
is the tragic mystery of our fate, and of all existence;
that others also should some day be manifested in other
worlds or to other spirits, would be a further decree of
fate; but that all should lie for ever in the realm of
essence is a luminous necessity raised far above any
accident of destiny or decree of power.   It could not
be otherwise.   If you deny that realm, you acknowledge it.   If you forget it, you consent that it should
silently laugh at you in your sleep.

# POSTSCRIPT

## CORROBORATIONS IN CURRENT OPINION

AFTER revolving these things in my mind for many years in intellectual solitude, when at last I was bringing this book to a close—not without profound disappointment that for all my labour it should be no better than it is—I have had the satisfaction of finding that quite independently, in the most various quarters, the same intuition is returning to the world. Not that in my own mind it needed confirmation: these are not eventual matters of fact on which testimony is needed or witnesses are to be counted like so many head of cattle; but after all, a book is addressed to the public, and the impulse towards expression and communication would remain abortive if no one was ready to listen or to understand. True, my doctrine was neither new nor extinct. Platonism was still remembered; round the corner, though strangely out of sight, there was always Catholic philosophy; and far away Indian philosophy loomed impressively in its unravelled labyrinth. But the notion of essence in these systems seemed to be either incomplete or impure, or both impure and incomplete: they were accidental traditional faiths borrowing from logic such helps or extensions as they could welcome; they had not that honest personal seat nor that fearless outlook which amid so many weaknesses made the strength of modern philosophy. My allegiance is rather to the earlier Greeks, who looked freely and ingenuously on the universe with the curiosity of children, but of children bred nobly and protected from false terrors by a manly civilisation. The autonomy of reason which they so beautifully and simply achieved is not to be surrendered. In part, indeed, it had been recovered by the modern mind, in its romantic Protestantism; but without the Greek clearness and inner freedom. The British and German schools in which it

had been my fate to be educated, were themselves obscurely
rooted in religious confusions. For three hundred years they
had hardly been able to distinguish the universe or the realm
of essence from the vapours of animal feeling.

Of late, however, various rifts or transparencies have
appeared in the low sky of subjectivism; and curiously, it is
the realm of essence that seems to become visible first—the
stars, as it were, before the sun. Matter, though so much
nearer and dearer to the heart of mankind, is even harder to
define and to situate from a psychological point of view; for
the more "objective" a psychological idealist wishes to render
his "realities", the more empirical and sensualistic they must
become: in other words, the more subjective. If an idea
develops within its bosom a theory of its own origin or environment, it remains a mere idea more elaborate than it was, but
not more cognisant of anything beyond; whereas if it is satisfied
to contemplate and to define its internal theme or quality, it
thereby begins to dominate a field of logical relations independent of its momentary attention or existence. Thus
intelligence, like the dove after the Flood, escapes from the
Ark of subjectivism more easily through the window than
through the door.

Three recent descriptions of the realm of essence, one
English, one German, and one French, lie at this moment
before me. Perhaps a brief report of them may serve to
convince the reader that in all this I am not dreaming alone,
but that on the contrary I am introducing him to an eternal
background of reality, which all minds when they are truly
awake find themselves considering together.

1. In a volume entitled *The Concept of Nature*, by A. N.
Whitehead, a systematic distinction is drawn between "events"
on the one hand—which is the name there given to all self-
existing facts or portions of nature, and on the other hand
"sense objects" and "scientific objects"—which are the names
given to essences, or at least to such essences as the author is
concerned with. That he should recognise essences clearly,
yet should call them by names so adventitious to their intrinsic
nature, is an anomaly easily explained by the circumstances.
Whitehead is primarily a mathematician, naturally at home
amongst essences; but he is an Englishman, and was drawn
toward metaphysics at a time and in a circle in which an

intense local reaction was taking place in British philosophy in favour of realism, but of a realism that should be still empirical and moralistic. It is characteristic of British reformers to disown the distressing consequences of some traditional principle, in order to be free to cling to it with a happier mind; and as an Anglican Catholic must denounce the Pope, so an Anglican realist must eschew matter. Here the traditional principle was that of Berkeley, that the only objects of know-ledge are inert ideas, or the immediate data of experience; and the distressing consequence was that in that case nothing latent or dynamic could exist in nature or could be made an object of study. This consequence, at first blush, had seemed to Berkeley a palmary argument for religion, and later it was deliberately made the corner-stone of transcendental idealism; but it was wormwood now in the mouths of the new realists, engrossed as they were in dogmatic judgement, in mathematics, and in cosmological physics. Might not this consequence be denied, while maintaining that principle, if we alleged that things are in reality compacted of ideas, of "objects" immedi-ately given in experience but existing independently of know-ledge? All would then be reality and nothing appearance, yet nothing would exist otherwise than just as it appeared. Events, or the substantial facts in nature, would be concretions of human "sense objects" and of human "scientific objects"; they would no longer be free to embody, to the confusion of sense and science, any essences whatsoever which the Creator might have wished them to possess.

How these human "objects" enter into events and compose them I will abstain from inquiring; suffice it that in themselves these "objects" are evidently essences and not existing elements. Whitehead continually calls them "eternal objects"; and that is final. Nothing can be more opposite to an event, or more remote from natural existence, than any eternal being. Yet that the *terms*—not indeed the intended *objects*—of sense and science are eternal essences could not escape so accomplished a mathematician. In his early collaboration with Bertrand Russell, at a time when the latter shared with G. E. Moore a virgin enthusiasm for ideal entities, Whitehead could daily measure the gulf which separates the realm of logic from that of fact. It was a saying of his in those days—for youth some-times has a shrewdness denied to distracted age—that some truths could be proved but were unimportant, and others were important but could not be proved.  Logic evidently was never quite satisfying to this logician;  even while feeding on its manna, he yearned for the flesh-pots of fact.  Tastes are free; but as the whole virtue of flesh-pots is to be eaten, so the whole virtue of events is to be enacted; an effort to describe the cuisine of nature exhaustively, were success in it possible, would yield dreadful literature and no food.  If, nevertheless, any one had a desire for such preternatural knowledge, would he be likely to attain it by overlaying the current cook-book of science, which after all has a relative validity, with rich metaphysics of his sheer invention?

In a later book on *Science in the Modern World*, Whitehead has distinguished essences even more clearly from the occasions on which they may be realised.  "Each eternal object," he tells us, "is an individual which, in its own peculiar fashion, is what it is."  "Each eternal object is just itself, in whatever mode of realisation it is involved.  There can be no distortion of the individual essence without thereby producing a different eternal object."  "Thus actualisation is a selection among possibilities."  Each "is systematically and by the necessity of its nature related to every other eternal object".  "The realm of eternal objects is properly described as a 'realm', because each eternal object has its status in this general systematic complex of mutual relatedness."  "A limited set of such objects is itself an eternal object; it is those eternal objects in that relationship."  "Thus the complexity of an eternal object means its analysability into a relationship of component eternal objects."  "An eternal object, such as a definite shade of green, which cannot be analysed into a relationship of components, will be called 'simple'."

The nature of essence could hardly be recognised more frankly: it is eternal, compacted of internal relations, indifferently simple or complex, and at every level individual.  It composes an infinite pure Being.  If there are impurities in Whitehead's description they arise, not from his conception of the field of essence itself, where his mathematical expertness gives him an enviable scope and fertility, but rather from refraction in the thicker atmosphere through which he approaches it.

2. Entirely free from these entanglements, though perhaps caught in others, is the view of essence contained in the *Pure*

*Phenomenology* of Edmund Husserl.[1]    He is an analytic psychologist of the most conscientious systematic kind, never for-
saking the plane of reflective autobiography; and to boot he is
a convinced transcendental idealist, always remembering the
activity of thought involved in the contemplation or definition
of any object; so that his theory is like those early maps of the
known world in which the geographer, proud of his young art,
placed in the foreground a representation of the compass,
sextant, and telescope, which had served him in his construction; while in another part, to fill in some large tract of *terra
incognita*, he might show us the gallant ship in which he made
his voyages of discovery, or a group of the naked savages found
at the antipodes.    Such marginal decoration is not without its
charm; and the modern reader, accustomed to romanticism
even in philosophers, may be more willing to look on essence
if he is told at the same time that he is looking at it, and how
the vision has been achieved.    Autobiography may be enlightening even in logic: it reminds us that our map is a map;
but it is also grotesque, since it is not the map's business to
describe cartography; and thought turns towards essence for
the sake of essence, not for the sake of thought.    Yet there are
advantages in this circumspection or contortion; it is not so
easy in learned Germany as in England or America for the gay
philosopher to ignore transcendental criticism and psychological fact simply because they were known to some past
generation, or because they annoy him and he is interested in
something else.

Husserl accordingly professes to study "phenomena",
which the Platonic tradition identifies with appearances and
the positivistic tradition with events; and we might doubt for
a moment whether he is considering essences at all, and not
rather facts or existing objects.    But no: all the emphasis falls
on the word *pure*; objects, in order to enter the realm of this
phenomenology, must be thoroughly *purified*.    This purifica-
tion consists in reducing the object to its intrinsic and evident
character, disregarding all question of its existence or non-
existence, or of its locus in nature; or, in my language, it
consists in suspending animal faith, and living instead con-

---

[1] *Ideen zu einer reinen Phänomenologie und phänomenologischen Philo-
sophie*, von Edmund Husserl ; Halle, 1922.    I translate the thankless text
rather freely for the reader's convenience, supplying the original phrases in
parentheses where fairness seems to demand it.

templatively, in the full intuition of some essence. This
essence may be as complex and as rich in inner perspectives as
imagination can make it; it may span any depth of specious
time, or intuited duration; every idea which science or faith
may turn into a creed, or use in the description of existence,
is in its spiritual immediacy a pure essence, a term given to
contemplation, distinct logically and æsthetically; otherwise
science and faith would be mere chatter, verbiage accompanying certain turns in action, not inner possessions or forms of
thought. Nothing is therefore removed from experience by
purifying it, except its distraction; and an essence, far from
being an abstraction from a thing, is the whole of that thing as
it ever can be directly given, or spiritually possessed. "Instead," says Husserl, "of setting up a natural world by a
transcendental act of naive assertion, and being driven by the
implications of that assertion to posit other transcendent things
one after another, we put all these positings aside, we refrain
from becoming accomplices in that act; and we direct our
discerning, scrutinising, contemplative glance upon the field
of pure intuition in its absolute intrinsic being. . . . We live
henceforth in these acts of supervening attention, ranging over
the infinite field of absolute immediacy—the bed-rock of
phenomenology."

"Geometry and phenomenology," we read in another place,
"being sciences of pure essence, lay down nothing concerning
real existences. Hence clear fictions will not only serve just
as well for these constructions as do actual perception and
experience, but often much better." "Pure or transcendental
phenomenology is not a science of fact but a science of essences
or forms. The phenomena of transcendental phenomenology
are in their nature non-existent (*characterisiert als irreal*). All
immediate data (*Erlebnisse*) transcendentally purified are non-
existent, and are situated out of all local relation (*Einordnung*)
to the 'real world'." "As the datum of personal experimental
perception is a particular thing, so the datum of intuition is a
pure essence." "Every science of fact or of experience must
needs draw the fundamental terms of its theory from some
formal ontology." "Immediate vision, not necessarily sensuous observation of things, but awareness yielding any original
datum, no matter of what quality, is the ultimate source of
validity for all rational assurance." "All that I believe to
exist in the world of things has, in principle, only a presumptive

existence." And finally, in answer to the inevitable reproach—as if it were a reproach!—of being a Platonist, the author says: "If 'object' meant 'existing object', and 'reality' meant 'existing reality', then indeed to call Ideas objects and realities would be to indulge in a perverse hypostasis; but when the two are explicitly opposed, and when 'object' is defined as any theme of discourse whatsoever, what can be the remaining objection?" "Between immediacy and existence yawns a veritable abyss in the quality of being (*Sinn*). Existence is posited in perspectives, never given absolutely as it is, and has an accidental and relative status: whereas being in the immediate is certain and unconditioned, and by its very nature not subject to perspective or given in an external view."

Such a firm adherence to transcendental principles serves to bring out the fundamental and ultimate part played by essence in knowledge, and its own immaterial and incorruptible nature; but perhaps this phenomenology is itself only an external view and a perspective, since the fact that experience must play with terms or essences does not imply that all essences must figure in experience. No doubt the field of *possible* intuition, the range of pure spirit, is infinite, and none other than the realm of essence itself; but is pure spirit itself possible, or does actual intuition realise all essences, or even as many as are realised in the unprobed structure of nature? A naturalist must be allowed to doubt it; and also to look for the genesis and meaning of immediate experience in the material and animal world, where a malicious transcendentalism, one that isolates mind in mind, cannot consistently look for them.

3. If a mathematical physicist can vindicate the eternity of essences, and a psychologist their purity, a pupil of the Oriental school may well vindicate their infinity; he will help to dissipate any lingering suspicion that they might be dependent for their being on human intuition or on embodiment in nature. In the books of René Guénon [1] the study of essence in its own absolute sphere is called metaphysics. The proper, and even the etymological, sense of this word, he tells us, "is that by which it designates whatever lies beyond physics, provided we understand by physics, as the ancients always did, the whole of all the sciences of nature". "Nothing can be metaphysical

[1] Especially *Introduction générale à l'étude des doctrines hindoues*, 1921, and *L'Homme et son devenir selon le Vedânta*, 1925.

except that which is absolutely stable, permanent, independent of all events and in particular of all historical circumstances." Metaphysics is the consideration of the universal, of the absolutely unlimited; not of matters which "special sciences may leave out because their present development is more or less incomplete, but rather of what, by its every nature, eludes the touch of these sciences." In the domain of metaphysics no experience, no contact with fact, is possible. "Being beyond physics, we are also, for that very reason, beyond experience ", that is, our thought is not intent on surrounding existences, but on the nature and relations of essences chosen and defined by that thought itself. "Hence, in questions of metaphysics, all that can change with times and places is merely the mode of exposition . . . that which is beyond nature, is also beyond change. . . . No discoveries are at all possible in metaphysics. . . . All that is discoverable may have been equally known by certain men in all ages: and such is, in fact, what we may gather from a profound examination of traditional metaphysical doctrines. . . . Metaphysics excludes hypothesis; whence it follows that metaphysical truths cannot be in the least doubtful in themselves; if there is ever occasion for discussion or controversy, it can only be on account of some defect in exposition or in comprehension." "Metaphysical truths can be conceived only by a faculty which, because its operation is on the immediate, we may call intuitive; if it be thoroughly understood that it has absolutely nothing in common with what certain contemporary philosophers call intuition, a merely sensitive and vital faculty properly inferior to discursive intelligence and not superior to it. . . . We speak here of intellectual intuition, which is necessarily infallible, not being actually distinct from its object. Such is the essential basis of metaphysical certitude"; whereas reasoning "is evidently fallible in consequence of its discursive and mediate character ".

This use of the term metaphysics would be unobjectionable, if it could be adhered to with constancy, and by general agreement: but metaphysics has always been, and is to-day, an attempt to establish truths about nature and existence otherwise than by observation, measurement, and experiment: nor am I sure that the Indians, and their French interpreter after them, do not attribute to their metaphysics any physical prerogatives, or to their intuition any feminine or Bergsonian privilege of being a miraculous substitute for intellect and a short cut to knowledge of fact. There is a sense, indeed, in which all existing things depend upon the non-existent realm of pure essence, since they could not be what they are, either intrinsically or in their internal relations to every other nature, did they not realise and illustrate some part of that primordial structure of being; so that any elucidation of pure essences explores a part of those essences one or another of which actual things must assume if they are to exist at all, or allow anything to be seen or said of them; but so long as the study of essences is *a priori*, imaginative and metaphysical, there is no likelihood or presumption that *those* essences will be found realised in anything existent. Before any such assumption can be made legitimate, we must turn with an absolutely docile and clear mind to the empirical aspects and relations of the facts themselves, as exploration and practical mastery unroll them before us; and then, when we have ascertained what essence, in some measure and in some respect, these existing things possess, we may freely develop the dialectical relations of that essence and deepen thereby our intellectual understanding of those things: as, for instance, has been done in mathematics to every one's satisfaction. But if arithmetic and geometry had not been originally the coinage of mechanical art, stamped upon the mind by commerce with things, they would have had no application to existence, and no authority over it—as indeed they have not over the whole field of psychic and moral being. Pure metaphysics, then, must call for aid on sense before it can claim to describe existence; it becomes impure and abusive, and such metaphysics as we are all accustomed to, when it presumes to describe nature without her consent. And can we doubt that Indian metaphysics does so at least as boldly as the metaphysics of the West? Else how comes it infallibly to distinguish five physical elements, neither more nor less, or to know that qualities of human sensation, such as sound, are intrinsic to those elements, or to assume the transmigration of souls, or to posit Ishwara and other existing deities between man and the impersonal infinite? Far be it from me to quarrel with the ideology of holy men; my wish is rather to understand and revivify as far as possible the essences which any spiritual tradition has made symbols of fate or themes for profound contemplation: my own native themes and symbols are probably not better. Only I would not let the lust of imposture, in others or in myself, distort that meditation. Delusion is the greatest enemy to peace.

How perfect such intellectual peace may ultimately become, how remote from all bias or presumption, appears in the direction of all Indian discipline upon deliverance from existence. Of course, this deliverance can be imaginative only, else peace would never be realised: but to exist as if not existing is a blessed deliverance, not only from the troubles of the flesh, but from the illusions of philosophy: it is the enlightenment which the philosopher seeks. Existence produces a false isolation and a vain reinforcement of some fragment of essence which by the logical necessity of its being forms part of an infinite and eternal realm. We therefore escape and overcome existence automatically in the act of understanding what existence is—that it is blindness to almost everything: although this blindness comes of being dazzled by a few features which matter, the principle of existence, happens to embody and to press upon the attention of the organisms which it forms.

The universe, then, is but a stain in the purity of the infinite,[1] of that non-existence by accident which is pure Being by necessity. Such bandying about of dark phrases need not irritate a tolerant mind, that knows the various realms of being in their disparate sorts of reality. Thus Guénon himself uses the word Being, not, indeed, for existence, but for only so much of essence as is illustrated there: precisely for that segment of essence which I call the realm of truth. "If ontology or the science of Being", he writes,[2] "is subordinate to metaphysics and belongs to it, it is far from identical with metaphysics as a whole: because Being does not signify the non-manifested absolutely, but only the principle of the manifested part"; that is, Being is so much of the eternal script as the reagent is destined to render visible at one time or another. "Consequently that which lies beyond Being is of much more importance metaphysically than is Being itself: in other words, it is Brahma, not Ishwara, that must be acknowledged to be the Supreme Principle."

According to this use of language, metaphysics would mean the description of the realm of essence, ontology that of truth, and physics or natural philosophy that of existence: existence

---

[1] "L'univers n'est qu'un défaut dans la pureté du Non-Être": Paul Valéry; *L'Ébauche d'un serpent*, in the volume of poems entitled *Charmes*.
[2] *L'Homme et son devenir*, p. 45.

N

having an urgent sort of reality, but a derivative and a lame sort. "Being, while it is properly the principle of universal manifestation", the essence which is temporally embodied in the universe, "lies outside and beyond this manifestation of it—and here we may call to mind the 'unmoved mover' of Aristotle." The existing world, as well as its eternal essence, "is no doubt real, but only in a relative fashion, by virtue of its subordination to its principle, and, in so far as something of this principle is reflected in it, as an image reflected in a mirror draws all its reality from the object, without which it would have no existence. But this subordinate reality, which is only borrowed, is illusory in comparison with the supreme reality" —that is, with the eternal essence there momentarily exemplified—"even as the image in the mirror is illusory in comparison with the object: and if we attempted to cut the image off from its original, the illusion would vanish into nonentity pure and simple"—for then, besides being unsubstantial and impermanent it would not even deceptively manifest any essence. "From this we may understand that existence, or conditioned and exemplified Being, is at once real in one sense and illusory in another; a point which people in the West have never rightly understood."

In invoking the authority of the Indians and of their lucid French interpreter, I wish I might invoke it without reserve; but there is a mass of cosmological and historical extravagance, entangled with their "metaphysics," which is nothing to my purpose. Tradition is venerable, where it transmits a unanimous spiritual discipline, by which the souls of essential hermits, in every age and country, have been made sensitive to the contingency of fact and the eternity and infinity of pure Being; but superstitions too are traditional, and not for that reason respectable. Superstition prevails also in traditional philosophy in the West, not only in theology, but in biology and psychology; it is maintained there by an ancient and stubborn confusion of formal with efficient causes. The forms which things wear, since these things could not be themselves without those forms, are said to *make* the things what they are; and so the essence by which a thing is classified and named is introduced among the efficient conditions which have ushered it into existence and endowed it with that particular form: conditions which are all ultimately material. Matter is requisite for continuity in change, or for brotherly existence.

This is often implied and sometimes confessed by the most sweeping idealisms: thus Guénon himself writes,[1] "Individual modifications, such, for instance, as pleasure and pain . . . all proceed from the plastic principle, *Prakriti* or *Pradhâna*, as from their only root. It is in this substance, containing potentially all the possibilities of manifestation, that the modifications are produced in the phenomenal order, by the mere unfolding of these possibilities, or, to use Aristotelian terms, by their passage from potentiality into act. 'Every modification (parinâma), says Vijnâna-Bhikshu, from the original formation of the world (that is, of each cycle of existence) until its final dissolution comes exclusively out of *Prakriti* and its derivatives.'" Whence, indeed, should change come, except from a region of changes? Where else should existence be enacted, save in a medium where forms may arise and lapse, may be irrationally conjoined, and may quarrel for their substance and transmit it to one another? The realm of essence, or a pure spirit eternally contemplating that realm, since it is immutable and incapable of any local emphasis or arbitrary exclusion, can have no influence whatsoever on the production of anything.

Nevertheless, bewildering equivocations continue to play about the word *make*. What makes this table a table? Surely, we may innocently answer, its form and its uses. Therefore, in contempt of the wood and the carpenter, the metaphysician may proceed to assure us that the essence of tabularity or the essence of utility is the true and only creator of this table. An air of profundity may be given to this nonsense by the fact that the genesis of things in nature is mysterious, and untraceable by human fancy; while we reconcile ourselves habitually to our own being and actions, merely by naming and expecting them. As within us, so without us, the flux of matter, amid a welter of waste and chaos, is rich in transitory harmonies; and this world is truly miraculous, in the sense in which any existing world was bound to be so. The verbiage of metaphysics might therefore pass as decent drapery for our ignorance or eloquent expression of it; but the trouble is that when some good critic detects that innocent imposture, he may extend his scorn to the realm of essence in its legitimate prerogatives. These do not include any power of piecing out the imperfections of physics; the forms of things conceived to exist

[1] *L'Homme et son devenir*, p. 69.

before the things and to call them into existence would, indeed, be *chimaerae bombinantes in vacuo.* Nevertheless the forms which things assume, when they assume or suggest them, are clearer, more interesting, and more beautiful than their substance or their causes. It would be a pity if the abuse of logic hardened men's hearts against poetry, and made them enemies to their own intellectual life. The metaphysicians, in their impatience of pure essences, which are their appointed food, are to blame for this misunderstanding: they insist that their clairvoyance is historical or physical knowledge; but this pretension is not only easily disproved, but is unworthy of their contemplative vocation. This expressly carries their thoughts beyond the accidents of life, and lifts them into communion with another realm of being, more akin to the spirit, since there an infinite variety, a boundless freedom, coincides with peace, and possession with security.

# INDEX

Abstraction not the principle of essence, 16, 32-40; incidental to discourse, 37

Aristotle, 62

Beauty arrests attention on essences, 8; is itself typical of essence, 152-154

Being eminently possessed by essence, 23, 24; contrasted with existence, 47

Being, Pure, is infinitely pregnant, 50; is positive and inclusive, 57; not identical with the idea of God, 58

Berkeley, 170

Buddha, xxii

Catholic philosophy, v, 168

Complexity no anomaly in nature, 141

Composition a physical process impossible in essences, 138-140, and Chapter X. *passim*

Contemplation suspends faith, 6. Cf. *Intuition*

Dante, xviii, 114

Dasgupta's *History of Indian Philosophy*, xxii

Descartes, 159, 160, 164

Dialectic moves among essences, 3; its basis biological, 89-91, and Chapter VII. *passim*; its transitions not essential, 96; a mode of moral integration, 99-107; its issue intuition, *ibid.*

Error, 2, 124-126

Essence, use of the word, 33; the realm of, described, viii, 24; indestructible, 57, 167

Essences, their part in knowledge of facts, viii, ix; not temporal or dynamic, 15; non-existent, 21; real even when not manifested, 22-24; often not beautiful, 30; not substances, 31; not abstractions, 16, 32-40; not constituents of things, 43, 44; inhuman, 72, 92; their unity or integration, 147; better than things, 179, 180

Eternity proper to essences, 24, 25, 170

Euclid, 105

Exemplification and alternative terms, 121 *note*; how it may be imperfect, 123

Existence, competitive, xviii; irrational, 21; temporal, 25; eludes intuition, 48, 93; is a surd, 109, 119

Extension an essence, not a substance, 149-151, 159, 161

Feeling is intuition of simple essences, 146

Finitude necessary to existence and value, xiv

Flux, cf. *Existence*

Free-will, 80

General terms such only in use, 36, 93; their biological support, 97

God sometimes identified with pure Being, xxii, 45; but distinct from it, 58-64, 162-164, 176

Guénon, R., 174-179

Happiness fixed on essences, 11

Hegel, 75, 84, 144; alluded to, 33, 34, 46, 53, 68-69

Heraclitus, 75

181

THE END

CPSIA information can be obtained
at www.ICGtesting.com
Printed in the USA
BVOW06s1809051217
501855BV00006B/206/P